P9-AQO-296

Northwestern University

STUDIES IN *Phenomenology & Existential Philosophy*

Laughing and Crying

Helmuth Plessner

Translated by

With a Foreword by

Laughing and Crying

A Study of the Limits of Human Behavior

JAMES SPENCER CHURCHILL

and MARJORIE GRENE

MARJORIE GRENE

NORTHWESTERN UNIVERSITY PRESS

EVANSTON 1970

Originally published in German under the title
*Lachen und Weinen: Eine Untersuchung
nach den Grenzen menschlichen Verhaltens.*
Third edition, copyright © 1961 by
A. Franke AG Verlag, Bern.

Library of Congress Card Catalog Number: 70–123611
ISBN: 0–8101–0321–4
Printed in the United States of America

James S. Churchill is professor of philosophy
at Purdue University at Fort Wayne.

Marjorie Grene is professor of philosophy
at the University of California at Davis.

Contents

Foreword

PHILOSOPHERS have always been given to speculating about the nature of man, usually about his uniqueness, sometimes about his want of uniqueness. But whatever their attitude or interest, they have nearly always focused their attention on man as knower, man as doer, man as speaker, or sometimes, man as maker. There is a whole area of human uniqueness which has been for the most part neglected, that is, the area of non-linguistic expression, whether in facial grimace or in bodily bearing and movement. Where expression has been treated as such, it has usually been in the Darwinian mood of reducing what looked to be human monopolies to their animal forerunners. But the range and subtlety of human expressiveness as such has had little investigation. It has seemed to philosophers, if they have thought of it at all, to be peripheral to the more central questions of knowledge or action.

Helmuth Plessner has long been interested in this neglected theme. In this little book he takes a particularly significant pair of types of expressive behavior, laughing and crying, and considers them both in themselves and in their relation to the fundamental nature of man. Laughing and crying are not "intentional" actions, like speaking, walking, or tacitly giving a sign, say, nodding one's head or smiling in assent. They belong, I suppose, to the Aristotelian class of "involuntary actions." Yet neither are they the sort of thing that other animals do; only human beings laugh and cry. Is this just an accident of our glandular and muscular makeup, or does it mean something in relation to the nature of man's existence as a whole? Plessner opts emphatically for the second alternative. He sees in these two phenomena a unique expression of our nature, or better, a breakdown of that nature which characteristically exposes it at its limits.

All animals both are and have bodies. Man both is and has a body, and knows it. But that is not to say with the rationalists that what characterizes man essentially is some kind of theoretical knowledge, some kind of "reason," which other animals do not possess. Nothing new is added to man in any substantive way, to distinguish him from other animals. The difference is in a relation: the relation of the living thing to its body. Animals live out of the center of their bodily being and cannot escape it. Their actions are at once absorbed into their bodily existence. Men too are animals; they live and experience out of and into the center of their bodily lives. But they *are* also the center itself in a way which is not the case for other animals. In the human case, life out of the center becomes reflexive: it sets itself to itself as its own. True, man cannot free himself from his own centered, animal existence; yet he has placed himself over against it. This Plessner calls "the eccentric position" of man. A living thing exhibiting this structure is still bound by its animal nature, yet detached from it, free of it. Its life has its natural place, as all animal existence has, yet is at the very same time detached from locality. It is everywhere and nowhere. Nor is there any new entity which comes from outside to create this situation—like Aristotelean νοῦς. There is only a new hiatus, a break in nature, which produces a new unity. In man "the living thing is body, is in its body (as inner life) and outside the body as the point of view from which it is both (body and inner life)." Only individuals characterized by this threefold structure, Plessner argues, should be called *persons*. The person is "subject of its experience, of its perceptions and its actions, of its initiative. It knows and it wills."

As persons, then, we stand at a double distance from our own body. We are still animals, but in a peculiar way. For we have not only an inner life distinct from, though not separable from, our physical existence; we stand over against both of these, holding them apart from each other and yet together. It is our eccentric position that gives to our existence the ambiguity, of necessity and freedom, contingency and significance, which it characteristically displays.

Laughing and crying, Plessner believes, constitute unique expressions of the breakdown of this eccentric position. It is when things are too much with us that we cry—even when we cry for joy. It is when the ambiguity in our fundamental situation breaks forth in such a way that we can't control it—and yet not in such a way that it harms us—it is in such a situation that we laugh. Plessner elaborates this basic theme in a number of subtle ways, and also invokes and criticizes the literature, anthropological, psychological, and in part philosophical, that is available on this double topic; but his central theme is the one just stated.

It is difficult to place this work in any particular pigeonhole of philosophical literature. Indeed, Plessner himself, in his introduction, disavows any such exercise. It may, however, help American readers to find their way if we label it as belonging to that branch of philosophy known on the continent of Europe as "philosophical anthropology." Indeed, it is a classic in this field. But, the reader may well ask, what is philosophical anthropology? On the map of contemporary philosophy, it is hard to locate. As Plessner rightly insists about his own study, it belongs neither to any special empirical -ology nor to any special philosophical -ism. Philosophical anthropology is a philosophical study of the nature of man. But as Wilfred Sellars has put it, "the aim of philosophy, abstractly formulated, is to understand how things in the broadest sense of the term hang together in the broadest possible sense of the term" (Wilfred Sellars, *Science, Perception and Reality* [London: Routledge & Kegan Paul, 1963], p. 1). Thus although a philosophical study of man may use psychology, neurophysiology, physical and social anthropology, sociology, it *is* none of these. Nor does its perspective belong to any one philosophical school. In a way it resembles phenomenology, for its aim is description rather than argument, insight rather than analysis. But it entails no method of reduction, no intuition of essences, no claim to apodicticity. Plessner's source in this little book, he says, is just "experience." And by this he means not the abstract units of sense or feeling of traditional empiricism but simply everyday experience in the most ordinary and comprehensive sense. The sciences of man, poetry, painting, ordinary encounters of man with man: all this may be grist for the writer's mill. Wherever he can find it he will garner insight into human nature: in this case into that strange pair of human monopolies, laughter and tears.

MARJORIE GRENE

University of California, Davis
November, 1969

Laughing and Crying

For Casper Ras
and Baukje Ras-Heerema

Preface to the Third Edition

Two works on laughing and crying could not be taken into account in the second edition since they appeared simultaneously with it: Alfred Stern's *Philosophie du rire et des pleurs* (Bibl. de Philos. Contemp.) (Paris, 1949), and Francis Jeanson's *Signification humaine du rire* (Paris, 1950). Stern, who was inspired by Bergson, approaches the phenomena from the standpoint of value and disvalue. Jeanson, although a follower of Sartre in outlook and method, arrives at the same moral and philosophical standpoint: human phenomena must be considered from the perspective of value to which every human being subjects himself. (See the excellent critique by S. Strasser, "Anthropologische Beschouwingen over Lachen en Wenen," *Tydschrift voor Philosophie,* XV [1953], in which he compares Jeanson's inquiries with my own.) The psychophysical problematic plays no role for these two French authors. For Stern, the representative of an older generation, it is a matter of psychic reactions: the anthropological question is still veiled by the psychological dimension. Jeanson, on the other hand, has already passed beyond this problematic before he begins. He is an existentialist, and pursues his quite arbitrary explications on the basis of a human existence [*Dasein*] already immune from separation into bodily and mental dimensions: on a pretheoretical level of irresponsible moralizing, from a position perhaps also suitable for the aims of *verstehende* psychology.

I should not neglect to mention that—also in 1950, the year in which the second edition was published—I followed Kunz's suggestion and included the phenomenon of smiling in my analysis. This work first appeared in the *Festschrift* for van der Leeuw. In 1953 it was included in my selected essays and lectures, *Zwischen Philosophie und Gesellschaft* (Bern).

H. P.

Preface to the Second Edition

WITH ONE AUSPICIOUS and one drooping eye, as befits the case, I again send out into the world this book, which was first published in 1941 and has been out of print for eight years. I am thankful that, despite these unauspicious times in the Netherlands and in Switzerland, the book has not lost its attraction for reader, publisher, or, let us hope, for the critics as well. I would have been happy to take more account of thoughts and suggestions from the latter, especially van der Leeuw, Binswanger, Kunz, and Portmann. But I must abstain, lest—to speak with Jean Paul—the water level of annotations rises to a menacing height. With van der Leeuw ("Grenzen van menschelyk gedraf," *Alg. Ned. Tydschr. v. Wysbegeerte en Psychologie,* XXXVI [1942]) I know that I am in complete agreement. Possibly my concept of eccentricity [*Exzentrizität*] makes, within the framework of this study, a more static impression than van der Leeuw's concept of abstraction in his *Der Mensch und die Religion* (Basel, 1940). This cannot be avoided, however, inasmuch as the former concept is also intended to bring into view man's concrete bodily existence, for which the possibility of detachment from the body (and herewith the path to the control of bodily organs, to the limit of total self-possession) must be shown to be constitutive, *even* in its purely somatic expressions. Those who know my *Stufen des Organischen und der Mensch* (Berlin, 1928), forgotten since 1933, will concur with me in this. There I settled accounts with Cartesianism.

On the other hand, I am not in accord with Binswanger's critique, which is oriented entirely to method (*Schweizer Archiv für Neurologie und Psychiatrie,* XLVIII, No. 1 [1941]). It cannot be answered even in terms of a philosophical anthropology, but only in a philosophy of anthropology, which must afford at the same time a critique of phenomenology. As a former student of Husserl, I am familiar with the misgivings of phenomenologists with regard to "theory." Binswanger is quite right; a strictly phenomenological analysis of human existence must reject concepts such as "attitude toward the body" as "constructions," not taken from man's actual self-interpretation. And there is no doubt that a self-disclosing description of the full import of human existence of the kind that Binswanger desires and carries out, a description which confines itself within the horizon of this existence, attains what descriptive psychology earlier aspired to but was unable to attain with the ontological technique at its disposal, namely, the explication of the matter-of-course [*des Selbstverständlichen*]. Similar tendencies are also apparent in Sartre and Merleau-Ponty. To understand a phenomenon means, in *this* dimension, to *take it back* into the particular context of meaning from which it arose. Does not Binswanger himself really see this when he holds that the question whether I have succeeded in understanding (or explaining?) laughing and crying as limiting cases of human behavior is answerable only on the basis of a newly elaborated theory? I take heart from Binswanger's acknowledgment that I was the first to advance a theory of laughing and crying—and now await the second.

I was tempted to follow the suggestion of Hans Kunz (*Basler Nachrichten,* December 28, 1941) and specifically include the phenomenon of smiling in my account, but I had to resist the temptation. Smiling is a mode of expression *sui generis.* It is (1) a germinal form, a braking form, and a transitional form for laughing and crying, thus, a mimic * expression surrounded by nonmimic expressions; (2) an expression "of" *and* gesture "for" an incalculable profusion of feelings, sentiments, attitudes, modes of social intercourse, and states or conditions, such as civility and awkwardness, superiority and embarrassment, compassion, understanding, indulgence, stupidity and cleverness, gentleness and irony, inscrutability and candor, repulsion and enticement, astonishment and recognition; (3) a gesture of pre-

* "Mimic"—pronounced *mīmic,* formed from "mime"—is used here as an English rendering of *mimisch,* "silently expressive," as in "mime," but "spontaneous." There is *no* connotation of "mimicry" or "imitation."—M. G.

tense ("Keep smiling from East Asia to America") * which says everything and nothing, the representative gesture *par excellence,* to this extent an exemplar of eccentricity as the unbridgeable gap between man and himself. In a word, I would have had to add a chapter to the book which would have widened its compass, and I feared this would weaken its impact. Perhaps I was wrong; in that case I hope in the third edition to be able to make up for the omission.

I have dealt in the Notes with Adolf Portmann's observations in his *Biologische Fragmente zu einer Lehre vom Menschen* (Basel, 1944) and "Die Biologie und das Phänomen des Geistigen" (*Eranos-Jahrbuch,* XIV [1946]).

For the rest, I have assimilated, in addition, some of the older and some of the more recent literature; on the other hand, I have made no changes in the text. At this point, I should also like to express my sincere thanks to my critics and my publisher, Dr. Lang in Bern, for their confidence in me.

Our idea of what is common to all men and differentiates them from other beings adheres—within the framework of familiar types of physical appearance and posture—to certain modes of behavior which are capable of development and which facilitate the intellectual and historical existence of man on whatever level or interpretation of culture you will: *speaking, acting methodically,* and *shaping things in various ways* [*variables Gestalten*]. Strange to say, however, our conception of the human monopolies deals as well with two forms or, indeed, outbursts, of an elementary character, incapable of higher development: *laughing* and *crying.* No reference to their lack of utility and the various ways in which we may find them offensive can dissuade us from thinking that a creature without the possibility of laughing and crying is not human. No attempt, however ingenious, to find instances of laughing and crying among animals can overcome our mistrust of them and release us from the duty of clarifying what laughing and crying really mean.

For this, as with all specifically human utterances, man himself must be heard. Only his grasp of these utterances, the interpretation which he gives them, the significance which he confers on them in the management of his life, reveals them in their

* The original reads: "Keep smiling *von Ostasien bis Amerika.*" —J. S. C.

full extent, and, what is more, all this belongs to them internally as their formative and impelling power. Any external registration of sound stimuli, of gesture and expressive movement [*Gebärde*],* misses the significance of laughing and crying, just as with speaking, acting, and shaping. Indeed, in the very selection of these particular kinds of behavior, which, however natural and innate in every human creature, distinguish this creature from nature, from animal existence—perhaps to its detriment and certainly with honor to another mode of existence—there already appears an interpretation of man by himself. In this interpretation, man lays claim to a special position which observation, directed merely to the externals of behavior by seemingly objective methods, can neither confirm nor contest.

Not only does the interpretation of man by himself enhance (or weaken), the gifts of speaking, acting, and shaping, as well as laughing and crying; not only does this interpretation give them different rank and significance (sacred or profane, for example); more to the point, it also singles them out from the rich store of human capability, elicits them from this store, is their first condition, the principle of their articulation and differentiation, and sees to it that they remain gifts which can be cultivated. Naturally, to the extent that human nature is corporeal, it admits of being determined by external characteristics, behind man's back, so to speak, and untroubled by any interpretation which man has of himself. But what is the significance of such characteristics as shape of the teeth, angle of vision, development of the cerebrum, differentiation of hands and feet, sparseness of body hair, or late puberty, irrespective of what a being so constituted does with these characteristics, irrespective, that is, of his behavior in the world? *Only behavior explains the body,* and only modes of behavior such as speaking, acting, shaping, and laughing and crying, all of which are peculiar to man in conformity with his apprehension and positing of goals, make the human body intelligible, complete its anatomy.

It is an obvious error, suggested to us by our everyday habits, to believe that types of behavior are in themselves as differen-

* *Gebärde* is a much broader term than either "gesticulation" or "gesture." In addition to the meanings of these terms, its meaning includes that of such terms as "bearing," "appearance," and "demeanor." "Expressive movement" is generally employed here as the translation of *Gebärde* since no more nearly adequate expression is available.—J. S. C.

tiated from one another and as neatly structured as the organs by which they are brought about. This holds true neither for the differentiated kinds of specifically human behavior nor for those kinds common to both men and animals, such as running, jumping, sitting, lying down, grasping, attacking, fleeing, resting, waiting, lurking, etc., which are located in the vital sphere because they can take place over long periods even without conscious control. We must not forget that the names at our disposal for denoting actual modes of behavior, the situations and objectives in and for the sake of which they take place, and the fixed image of the parts of the body of which we make use entice us to the assumption of modes of behavior, articulated in themselves but entirely void of significance.

Physiology, which is an analytic science, speaks of the functions which characterize relatively isolated organs such as the heart, blood vessels, kidneys, intestines, and lungs. And physiology must speak in this way if it is to gain insight into the way such organs affect one another. To this extent, therefore, provisionally, it makes good sense to differentiate an effect bound to two or more organs as their function from behavior in which the *whole* organism, even though under the particular influence of definite organs, enters into association with the environment. But in both cases the principle of the division into particular, differentiated functions or kinds of behavior is to be assigned neither to the organism alone nor to the environment alone but to the bond between the two. In view of this, the fact that it is not always clear what is function and what is behavior should not astonish us. There must be transitions here. To which shall we assign, e.g., sleeping, yawning, breathing, blushing, and turning pale? We will meet this situation again with laughing and crying.

Nevertheless, in the case of human behavior, if it is not a question of merely biological modes of behavior but of those specifically reserved to man, we find in addition a peculiar dependence not found among animals, a dependence which goes beyond that holding between the environment and the organism. Animal behavior is composed of a chain of functions of which the animal makes use, but yet does not coincide with this. It is a reciprocal bond between the whole organism and its milieu. Human behavior is also all this but, beyond it, is at the same time a reciprocal bond between man and himself.

It is the self-interpretation of man by himself as man—and

we should not confuse this with personal self-evaluation—which differentiates behavior in this instance and therewith assigns to particular types their locus and significance.

The ability to speak, to act, and to shape means having, not merely definite organs, but a meaning as well at our disposal, and also relying on this power. A self-disclosure, an appreciation of meaning, always precedes and guides mouth and hand, the "relation" of a person to his body and to the world in which he finds himself. As we shall see, speaking, acting, and shaping, also laughing and crying, are not rigid faculties which do their work secretly and exert power over a man whether he will or not. They are faculties only to the extent that man is completely at home with them and consents to them. A basic discovery, a basic invention, always precedes: a sustaining conception, that of being human—self-determining, responsible, capable of acknowledgment. Whatever is to be reckoned among the specific endowments of human nature does not lie in back of human freedom but in its domain, which every single individual must always take possession of anew if he would be a man.

Without this insight, we would never arrive at a theory of human behavior but would always be slipping back into the errors of the anthropologists and natural law theorists of those periods which thought abstractly, absolutistically, and unhistorically. Not only do men change; what is human is also altered in the changing course of time. All those fine catalogues and models of hereditary factors, faculties, and drives, by means of which we try to capture man and his behavior, from the point of view of social psychology, characterology, or typology, remain only makeshift jobs. For such catalogues have too little grasp of the dependence of their concepts and types on the idea which they, the investigators, and they, their objects, have of themselves: the dependence of behavior on the sense which awakens it to life and form.

Nevertheless, man does not form himself according to his own image or according to that of a superior being alone; "Es bleibt ein Erdenrest / Zu tragen peinlich": "An earthly part remains, painful to bear." * Here, in the conflicts with his corporeality, man experiences a limit which defies all spiritual and historical change. As far as man's altercation with his body extends, and there is no speaking, acting, or shaping without

* Goethe, *Faust,* Pt. II, ll. 11954–55.—M. G.

this, it remains in the shadow of his cumbersome anatomy, as the compass of the universally human. The how, what, or whereof of our speaking, acting, or shaping: that changes because it belongs to the spirit, which, in historical action, must be constantly reconquered; it belongs to comprehension, to goal-setting, to appraisal. But the modes of speaking, acting, and shaping, often overlapping and uniting in a common task, are preserved in all change.

So also laughing and crying. If it is correct, and if the following investigation succeeds in demonstrating, that laughing and crying are forms of expression of a crisis precipitated in certain situations by the relation of a man to his body (a relation which is a form of behavior as well and not a piece of fixed machinery on which one need only rely), then laughing and crying are revealed as genuine, basic possibilities of the universally human, despite all historical change, all varieties of jest, wit, drollery, humor, irony, pain, and tragedy. Laughing and crying are sensitive reagents, which literary artists, their true masters and teachers, know how to use. Our analysis has much to learn from them. And yet, to comprehend the origin of laughing and crying, we must look to the basic form of human existence under the spell of the body. As Stendhal suggested (he mentions only laughter, we add crying), "le problème du rire doit être écrit en style d'anatomie et non en style d'académie."

Introduction

MUCH HAS BEEN WRITTEN ABOUT LAUGHING, little about crying. The theme laughing *and* crying is among the exceptions. This asymmetrical division of interests in an obviously symmetrical association of phenomena has traditional grounds. Neither laughing nor crying itself was a matter of discussion, but its motive, not the form of expression in its singularity compared to other forms of expression such as speech, gesture, and expressive movement, but its occasion. For the most part, theoretical writers have directed their attention to the question of what we laugh at and why we cry, toward the aesthetic and psychological laws of the amusing and the sad, the comic and the tragic. In their studies, laughing and crying played the role of indicators which report the course of a reaction. Their analysis is concerned with the reaction and treats the indicators only as means.

Those familiar with the history of psychology and aesthetics will better understand the asymmetrical division of interest, the preference for laughter, and the neglect of crying. Both these disciplines throughout their history, i.e., since they developed a consciousness of the interrelation of their problems (and this consciousness hardly extends beyond the eighteenth century), have labored, inquired, and found answers under the thralldom of the concept of the mental image [*Vorstellung*]. This model of the mind as the stage for magic-lantern displays and peep shows accommodates itself more naturally to laughter, which is bound to images, than to crying, which is bound to feeling. The theory of crying, like the theory of feelings in general, necessarily suffered from the fact that the disciplines in question tried to adapt them to their model of the mind and were not capable of breaking free of the spell of consciousness as a so-called horizon of all experience.

Only in the last decades has the truth begun to be appreciated that the theory of knowledge does not enjoy a commanding position, that accordingly the perspective of consciousness and of mental images is only one among the many ways in which man moves in and with the real world. The originality of feeling, intuition, and conduct thus demands that they receive their own mode of interpretation. Philosophy and psychology share equally in this truth. What is more, this truth is the result of a revolution in the domain of all the disciplines concerned with man. The study of history and society has made them suspicious of rigid models and dissatisfied with an out-of-date theory of science. Thus they want to see the essence of human nature with new eyes. The revolution is directed against two dogmatic systems: idealism (primarily of the Kantian-Hegelian stamp), which is at home in the old world, and positivism of the Darwinian-Spencerian variety, which the Americans especially abandon only with reluctance. The work of Nietzsche, Bergson, and Dilthey is slowly being reabsorbed and forms, if not a new point of view, at least a new readiness to understand man spontaneously and radically as a living reality, or, what amounts to the same thing, to learn to see man with his own eyes.

An important, if not the most important, means to this end is the *theory of human expression.* The romantics had already recognized its significance, although by coupling it with speculative metaphysics they hampered its free development. With the energetic rejection of romanticism on the part of science, the turn to experiment, and—not to be overlooked—the development of comparative philology as an independent discipline, the theory of expression languished. However, there is one movement characteristic of the last decades which has awakened the theory to a new and promising life: that is the movement associated with the name of Klages, a movement opposed to the dominance of positivism and idealism. To Klages, in particular, is due the rehabilitation of and fresh impetus for the theory of expression, an impetus which has wider implications than his own theory and metaphysics.

Our study is in line with a theory of human expression. We wish to interpret laughing and crying as forms of expression. Their analysis no longer serves the aesthetics of the comic, of wit [*Witz*], of tragedy; it is not concerned with the psychology of humor and feeling but with the theory of human nature. The question reads: how are we to understand that a living creature of flesh and blood, which has speech and sign-making at its disposal—and thereby differs from animals—yet at the same time in its mimic expression documents its vital bondage and its kinship with animal nature? How is it possible that such a dual and intermediate creature can laugh and cry? How is it possible, in other words, what conditions must be given in order that such reactions can take place, reactions which, in the full sense at least, are reserved to man?

To assert that this study serves the theory of human expression means, then, that it aims at knowledge of human nature, provided, of course, that man's expression betrays something of this nature. And as long as we do not limit the concept of human nature to regions of man's existence which are foreign to expression, i.e., to an inwardness inaccessible to everything external and to all utterance, we should expect expression to be a mirror, indeed a revelation, of human nature. It certainly is such for the interplay of man with his body.

In our analysis of laughing and crying, the emphasis is on this interplay. Just as this analysis must necessarily occupy itself with the occasions of laughing and crying, whether emotional or conceptual, so it must also keep the interplay of the human person with his body constantly in view. Although the effect cannot be understood without the cause, the cause lies, not in the actual occasion alone, but just as much in the relation of man to his body, which always determines his existence in the world.

Our study does not, as is customary, evade the question of the physical form of expression of laughing and crying with a philosophical obeisance to physiology, and declare itself to be incompetent, but makes this form of expression the cardinal question and subordinates everything to its solution. With this approach it is continuing the line of my earlier efforts. The first [1] had as its object the interplay of the functions of communication or understanding and the senses; the second,[2] the relation between organism, body, and environment on the different levels of plant, animal, and human existence. It is no accident, then, if we consider the phenomena of human expression from the point of view of the relation between man and his body in order to understand these phenomena from this point of view and conversely, from the phenomena, to learn something about this relation.

With this, we assert once more our conviction that an understanding of human nature, if it is to press radically on into man's fundamental constitution—one may call it anthropology or existential philosophy or what you will—must (1) proceed from an understanding of expression in the richness of its various possibilities, and (2) make intelligible the intermeshing of the components of expression in their whole breadth, from the mental to the physical.

But does this imply a psychophysics of laughing and crying? Surely not, if the concept "psychophysical" is taken in the Weber-Fechner sense. This classical psychophysics proceeds from a strict and, as people long believed, clear-cut separation between physical and mental events, events which on closer examination turn out to be artifacts of an experimental arrangement. Now artifacts can still assert something about the reality from which they have been wrested by our intervention, if we are in a position to correct what they assert, i.e., to compare the assertion with reality. To inquire about the relations between the magnitude of a stimulus and the magnitude of the corresponding sensation—taking careful note of the ambiguities of the word "magnitude"—surely has its value. It is not directed to thin air; it is concerned with something. But what it is concerned with, and artificially isolates, on the side of the "stimuli" as well as of the "sensations," we know only from the reality to which the inquiry is directed.

Experiments of this kind are useful and instructive. But they constitute, not the upshot of our knowledge of the interplay of physical and mental factors, but a means, desirable under certain circumstances and for certain purposes, by which to learn something about this interplay. We can make allowances for the artificiality of the results, due to the question itself, to experimental interference, and to the unavoidable fictions arising from causal analyses, but we must remain conscious of this artificiality as measured against the original context of life.

This original context falls victim to every type of cognition which pledges itself to a determinate method of observation, be it physiological, psychological, or psychophysical. Methodological procedure always follows the path of isolation. Isolation, in turn, implies abstraction. If one knows what he has abstracted from in order to attain the isolation of particular "factors," this isolation will not conceal the original context. But science has frequently made the mistake of taking the abstraction on which it rests for ready cash, for reality itself, as if its basic concepts and fictions were themselves set like building blocks in the original context itself. Physiology, psychology, and, not least, "quantitative" psychophysics are constantly exposed to such illusions and succumb to them when they set up the requirement that knowledge of the object under investigation must begin with their methodology. Such science then forgets the original context from which the object in its very character as open to investigation had been extracted, in which it had been interrogated [*ab-gefragt*], and must be interrogated again and again. It then neglects a contact in and with the immediate reality which objectively precedes every methodologically isolating "specialized" science.

To understand laughing and crying as expressive phenomena, therefore, does not mean that we subject them first to the isolating techniques of psychological and physiological methodology and then to a subsequent correlative unification according to the principle of psychophysics. On the contrary; it means first and foremost to put them back into their original living context. It means first of all to keep them free from the usual separations into sharply contrasted regions of physical and psychological objectivity, in order to cultivate perception of and understanding for the fact that it is here a matter of human affairs, which take place in the domain of the human experience of life, of the behavior of man to man and of man to world. Those who would criticize us because in this study we do not dance attendance with tables, curves, and series of experiments and who would see in the dearth of questionnaires and photographs a dearth of exactitude should consider—as should the disillusioned lover of exact definitions—that the reason for this was not a deficiency but rather an excess of accuracy, something which many authors in this difficult field have neglected, to the detriment of the subject.

That physiology and psychology have a share in our question goes without saying, but as to how great this share is only vague notions prevail. Expression, as the transition from inner to outer, presents a problem to sciences which have after all been established by the separation of the outer (bodily) from the inner (mental). If, misusing the concept of psychology, one interprets the mind from the beginning *as* external ex-pression

[*Äusserung*], then, to be sure, the problem vanishes—for psychology. But not so for physiology. Precisely as the physiology of expression, it will always see to it that consciousness of the "unfathomable" in all external expression and embodiment of the "inner" does not disappear. Such concern is motivated, not by comprehension of this fundamental category of life, but by incomprehension, by a very wholesome and necessary restriction of the range of physiology to bodily processes as such.

To whatever -ology one assigns the theory of expression, moreover, whether to psychology, anthropology, or sociology, it should not be overlooked that the treatment of questions of the nature and possibility of types of expression is, methodologically speaking, unaffected. A consideration of the concepts employed in the study of expressive phenomena must precede any investigation of these phenomena in their actual multiplicity. Typology, characterology, graphology, physiognomics, and mimetics cannot facilitate or take the place of such a consideration. They will not put to the phenomena the question which interests us. This is their privilege, just as it is ours to ask the question of the essence and possibility of expression, a question which has been overlooked or made trivial by many, if indeed, through arbitrary extensions of the concept of mind or through metaphysical theses, it is not lost sight of altogether.

Can we escape such theses? Does not our question as to the character and possibility of expression—in this case of laughing and crying—arise only by reason of a definite metaphysical conviction? We speak of "essence" or "nature," of expression as a mirror, a revelation of the "essence" of man (at least as regards the domain of the interplay of man with his body). We stress that man's existence in the world is determined by the relation to his body, that the understanding of human nature is bound to the possibility of expression as a unity of intellectual, affective, and physical components.

In the eyes of the reader, the warning advanced against the usual appeal to the empirical sciences naturally makes us liable to be suspected of some kind of metaphysical purpose. Thus, he will read into the use of terms like "intellectual" and "affective," in contrast to "physical," an avowal of triadism and will expect an explicit declaration in favor of this triple-essence theory of human nature, as opposed to dualism and monism. He will suppose that in the concept "possibility" (of expression) lies a potency, the knowledge of which would be crucial. He will take exception to the concept of "essence" or "nature." In short, he will detect an appeal to occult sources in our keeping a distance from the empirical. How simple it is to brand someone a follower of some metaphysical theory if he does not explicitly declare himself against it!

There is no occasion for this. Our questioning is dedicated to no metaphysics; it appeals to none for an answer. We entrust our inquiry to experience, to which its object and its cognitive sources belong. In this context experience suffers no restriction in order to oblige a method, but requires complete openness in the everyday commerce of man with man and man with world. If (in resisting the monopolistic claims of psychophysics, physiology, and psychology to the problem of laughing and crying) we argued above that our endeavor was first and foremost aimed at restoring the phenomena in their original living context as befits human affairs, the same also holds in the defense against the monopolistic claims of metaphysics. Phrases like "relation of man to his body," "physical," "affective," "intellectual," appeal to the average understanding and should not be used to express more than they assert within this horizon.

Granted, without strict conceptual limitations. Of itself, this is a broad field. But if we entrust ourselves to everyday experience, we must put up with uncertainty. Loyalty to everyday intuition is paid for only with an elasticity in linguistic usage. "Definitionists" who take umbrage at this should never forget what price terminological clarity exacts. We are convinced that exactitude of definition—not exactitude of inquiry—at least in human affairs (in which we include laughing and crying), brings with it the danger of impairment of vision, of one-sidedness, and of distortion.

"Man" is not a being who understands himself in the same way among all peoples and at all times; he is historically bound, precisely in his original, everyday understanding. The idioms of the language that shapes his thought, poetic or prosaic, the language in which he "expounds" himself,* spring from no timeless ground. They are products of history, deposits of dead religions and metaphysical systems, as much as they are the apparel of living beliefs. And yet it is impossible to demand of knowledge that is oriented to the enduring-in-change, to the non-

* *sich auslegt.* One cannot render the pun in English.—M. G.

and trans-historical, that it should not entrust itself to the idioms of common speech, but should take refuge, for the sake of terminological clarity and stability, in an artificial language.

Antiquity and Christendom alike have contributed to words of common speech like "mind," "soul," "body," and "human being." Tracing the changes in their significance, however, can never replace the analysis of what is reflected in them. The organization of the stimuli and motives of our conscious life into categories like cheerful and sad, comic and tragic, ironic and satiric, humorous and witty, and so on, does not come about by chance but has its own history. But what these words mean and where they have their roots is revealed only in living social understanding. Thus the analysis of all human expression remains, despite its historical stamp, directed to "everyday experience," to the province of man's behavior to his world and to his like. Thus the analysis can never call the concepts and schemata of a metaphysic to its aid.

In our case, this reserve relative to metaphysical theories does not spring from hostility toward, or devaluation of, metaphysical thinking but only from the concern to free ourselves from prejudices which stand in the way of a solution to problems of expression. The worst enemy of the sciences is the laziness which justifies itself with a tradition or an allegedly definitive, well-established doctrine. For centuries the alternative of parallelism and interactionism in the doctrine of mind-body relations barricaded the analysis of expression. Antimetaphysical agnosticism had an equally inhibitory effect. Today, metaphysics is concealed behind evolutionary ideas and tries, in line with the positivists' program, to comprehend the phenomena of expression in particular, like all human affairs, in terms of historical development.

For the analysis of expression, the evolutionary point of view undoubtedly has a stimulating power. As long as it remains a point of view, the disciplines dealing with expression will derive benefit from it; historical linguistics in itself proves this. But development as a controllable alteration from germ to the mature form, and evolution as progress (according to naturalistic criteria if possible) are two different things. Empirical study of the development of a human mode of expression through all stages of personal maturation unearths facts without bringing us nearer to an understanding of the mode of expression itself. On the other hand, the interpretation of the stages and series of phases within the framework of any given idea of evolution or development—whether it derives from Hegel, Darwin, or Bergson—subjects them to the selection of metaphysical criteria before the interpretation itself has become clear about what it is that passes through these stages and phases. In order to understand how something develops, one must first have understood what it is supposed to be developing *into*.

On this account, every observation of the genesis of human expression—whether with purely empirical or metaphysical intent (and the latter can be given a biological or psychoanalytical, in any case a naturalistic or "antimetaphysical," complexion) —must proceed from an understanding of the expression in question itself. What use are derivations, e.g., verbal speech from cries, from expressive movements and gestures of particular emotions, from tendencies to onomatopeia, from communication drives, if we ourselves are not clear about the expressive significance of language, its possibilities and its limits? What use is the finest exposition or interpretation of the phase-sequence of laughing and crying if their own expressive significance remains obscure? It is certainly not a matter of indifference to know when and under what circumstances these reactions first appear in infants and how they are differentiated in the course of development. But it is certainly an illusion to consider the germinal forms and first stages more informative than the fully developed forms of maturity.[3]

Equating the elementary in the sense of the initial with the elementary in the sense of the fundamental has always made for confusion. What is first in time is not necessarily first in substantive importance. Evolutionary metaphysics believes it can set aside this simple thought, especially since Darwinism presented it with a suitable instrument to shape its metaphysical conception scientifically and to connect individual development with phylogeny. A great part of the science of man still lives by this conception, even that part which believes it has nothing more in common with Darwinism and naturalism. Especially in Anglo-Saxon countries, it is difficult for investigators to free themselves from this perspective. And because, now as much as formerly, the problem of laughing (and crying) has attracted the greatest number of workers in those countries—even more than in France—this methodological side of the subject deserves to be vigorously stressed.[4]

It has been said often enough: the program of so-called behaviorism, with its rigid restriction of behavior to visible movements and series of movements, and the mechanistic interpretation of these as reflexes, has hindered more than furthered the investigation of behavior. Scarcely less harmful has been the dogma of evolution. For "primitive" forms of expression like laughing and crying it is especially natural to attempt an explanation in terms of "archaic" reactions like screaming, terror, shock, etc., and to reduce them to comparatively elementary drives for shelter or communication, to affective reflex mechanisms, or directly to sensory excitations. Thus the investigation is directed from the first into unsuitable paths. Even if laughing and crying are forms expressing a disorganization of the human person, with which a lowering of level, a breakdown of differentiation, and a general coarsening is naturally connected, still, the presumption that, in laughing and crying, archaic strata of existence are breaking through remains completely speculative.

To understand laughing and crying as forms of expression means to proceed from man as a whole, and not some particular aspect which can be detached from the whole in quasi-independent fashion, like body, soul, mind, or social unit. Man is accessible to us as a whole, that is, as our fellow man, and we are accessible to ourselves, in the context of behavior, in commerce with our own kind and with the environment. We live in and by this context; it is, though of course in various historical forms, the basis of all experience. Thus forms of expression are forms of behavior toward others, toward oneself, toward things, events, and everything that people can encounter. These forms do not lie within the fenced-off area of a consciousness providing isolation from external reality, not in the inner or outer aspect of human existence, but rather athwart all these antitheses. For dogmatists of some "ism" or other, this may be a reason to consider them secondary structures, conglomerates, or fictions of subsidiary importance.

Such people are not to be convinced. We are addressing only those who are ready to face experience without prejudice, experience which has neither passed through the sieve of some special science nor asks what different philosophies of experience think about it. Such lack of bias, to be sure, is found all too infrequently. Even the reader who is bound to no particular scientific system is usually inclined to ask about the standpoint, the method, in a word, the rubric, under which he can classify the book. He doesn't reckon with the possibility of being brought by a book to independence of thought and vision. He wants "contributions to" something which already exists. A book about laughing and crying? Well, a "contribution to" psychology, anthropology, existential philosophy, philosophy of life! He sees trends, schools, relations of dependence, or of master and disciple. But he sees neither the thing itself nor the originality. "The true reader must be an extension of the author," said Novalis. "Only then do I show that I have understood a writer, when I can act in his spirit; when, without diminishing his individuality, I can translate and play upon him in multifarious ways." *

* Friedrich Novalis, "Fragmente und Studien," *Werke und Briefe* (Munich: Winkler-Verlag, 1955), p. 374. (Throughout the book, all translations are my own.)—J. S. C.

1 / The Relation of Man to His Body

1. The Problematic Nature of Laughing and Crying

Laughing and crying are forms of expression which, in the full sense of the words, only man has at his disposal. At the same time, these forms of expression are of a kind to which this monopolistic situation is in strange contrast. For one thing, they have nothing in common with language and expressive movement, by which man shows himself superior to other living creatures and which provide his thoughts, feelings, and intentions with an expression that mediates by pointing, that is objective and subject to discussion. Laughing and crying are not found in the same stratum, are not on the same level, as language and expressive movement. To laugh or cry is in a sense to lose control; when we laugh or cry, the objective manipulation of the situation is, for the time being, over.

The eruptive character of laughing and crying links them closely with movements that express emotion. Just as, when we are mastered and deeply stirred by feelings, their force is stamped on facial expression and gesture, so here also the cheerful or the sad, the laughable or the touching and affecting occasion gains the ascendancy and must discharge itself. Closer to the inarticulate cry than to disciplined, articulate speech, laughing and crying surge up from the depths of life bound to feeling.

Nevertheless, their form of expression separates them from emotional expressive movements. While anger or joy, love and hate, sympathy and envy, etc., acquire in the body a symbolic stamp which allows the emotion to appear in the expressive movement, the expressive form of laughing and crying remains opaque and, for all its capacity for modulation, is largely fixed in its course. From this point of view, laughing and crying belong to the same range of processes as blushing, turning pale, vomiting, coughing, sneezing, and other vegetative processes, largely removed from voluntary influences.

Again, in comparison to the reactions just mentioned, eruptivity and compulsiveness of the form of expression, coupled with a lack of symbolic character, also appear to be especially prominent in laughing and crying. As vocal expressions, they cannot well be overlooked in social life. They are not mere reactions to the actual situation like blushing, turning pale, and so on (which are limited primarily to the person who is ashamed or alarmed); but they direct themselves to the situation, even if perhaps involuntarily, and interrupt the normal course of life. Nor should we overlook the fact, perhaps also of significance here, that laughing and (to a lesser extent) crying are easier to induce voluntarily than are the reactions controlled chiefly by the sympathetic and parasympathetic nervous systems.

Further, if simply as uniquely human forms of expression of an opaque character, falling outside the circle of intelligibly transparent expressions in speech, expressive movement, and mime, laughing and crying naturally arouse attention, then this interest deepens when we look at the diverse situations that induce them. Like the expressive form itself, they too are strange and go beyond the limits of the ordinary. It accords with learned tradition to be especially concerned with these diversities. Philosophers have been enthralled since antiquity by the phenomena of the comic and the tragic, of the joke and of the sublime. The expression, in itself somewhat insignificant, of the living creature, man, moves here into the technical, and therefore truly humane, perspective of the laws of aesthetics. Only since psychology and physiology have existed have the other aspects of laughing and crying come into view: the sustaining or releasing emotions of cheerfulness, sadness, regret, shame, commiseration and compassion, embarrassment; the bodily expressive movements performed in accordance with their muscular coordination, their nervous and presumably also hormonal regulation.

Thus the disclosure of many-sidedness and its elaboration in different disciplines, methodologically distinct from one another, raises the counterquestion of the unity of the phenomena of laughing and crying. In contrast to the specialized approach of the aesthetician, the psychologist, and the physiologist, this unity also necessitates a methodologically unique approach. For here it is not a question of the product of a synthesis to be attained a posteriori, but of the original unity in which we live, a unity always kept in view by the aesthetician, psychologist, and physiologist, even if—according to the special interest of each discipline—in a biased way. Starting from this unity, we can then understand the interaction of the physical, psychic, and mental dimensions; but from the dimensions, mutually isolated, we cannot understand the mechanism of their unity.

About it we know. The statement made at the beginning, that evidently only man has laughing and crying at his disposal, but not the lower animals, states no hypothesis which can one day be disproved by observation, but a certainty. For we know that the concepts laughing and crying lay claim to the widest range of human behavior, to the context in which indeed the words "mind," "soul," and "body" are once and for all at our disposal. We say, indeed, that tickling can produce laughter, and we find the smile, for example, among chimpanzees: the mouth drawn wide, the giggling sound characteristic of pleasure. These, although perhaps not the products of reflex action, still, as expressive motions remaining in the sensory, vital sphere, are no more to be considered genuine laughter than the compulsive laughter of sufferers from certain brain disorders. To laughing (and to crying) belongs—and if not, the concepts are misplaced—the significant and conscious relating of an expression to its occasion, an expression which breaks out eruptively, runs its course compulsively, and lacks definite symbolic form. It is not my body but I who laugh and cry, and for a reason, "about something." Whereas in bearing and expressive movement I immediately assimilate the occasion in a symbolic expression and thus dispose of it by a direct reaction, in laughing and crying I keep my distance from it: I reply to it.

Thus our problem is not to derive these specifically human forms of expression from the essence of human nature, for whatever is hidden in that essence is also contained in laughing and crying and gives us assurance of their humanity. Our problem looks different: it asks how their form of expression can be joined with human nature, as displayed in other specifically human powers, e.g., language and work. The relation to intelligible order which man lays claim to and attests by his activity must somehow also make laughing and crying possible; otherwise, the comic and the tragic, the funny and the sorrowful, could not have the effects they do. The matter under discussion is not whether laughing and crying are human monopolies, but how. The strangely opaque mode of expression of the human body must be understood from the relation of man to his body (and not, for example, from the problematic "relation" of mind to matter, of soul to body, as isolated entities).

Naturally, this task demands just as much a specific conception of human nature as a specific characterization of its bodily situation. Usually, if human monopolies are in question —language, the invention and use of tools, clothing, habitation, and custom—we are satisfied with a reference to rationality or intellectuality and somehow or other try to ground the human in these. Even our permanently erect posture, with its liberation of the hands, unburdening of the head, and broadening of the field of vision and distance to the environment, fits into this context. Everyone knows what man has in this monopoly and understands the link with the traditional criterion of his uniqueness: reason, mind. But what laughing and crying have to do with man and why exactly they are denied to other creatures remain obscure. In itself, their eruptive, compulsive, and inarticulate character resists any connection with reason and mind and points in the direction of the subhuman, which is nourished by affective sources alone. On the other hand, if laughing and crying were only affective utterances and emotional expressive movements, it would be incomprehensible why at least those animals most closely related to man cannot also laugh and cry.

Knowledge of the reasons which, under certain circumstances, dispose man to express himself in one way and not another also provides the answer to the question why only he and no other creature can so express himself. The presupposition of such knowledge is, above all, an unprejudiced view of the phenomenon in the wealth of all its aspects: the mental, the psychic, and the physical, and also, as far as method goes, a unique approach to it. We will not reach our goal via the well-trodden paths of biological interpretation or those of motivational or social psychology. Let us leave undecided whether laughing and crying are processes which serve a hidden purpose. Nature, the life of instinct, and society doubtless have a share in them. But we are, unfortunately, unacquainted with it, and hence it appears to us basically absurd to entrust the problem wholly to one of these anonymous powers. Nor do we get very far with causal explanations: we seem at once to be stuck fast in the breach between psychic or mental motive and physical effect.

Before one tries to interpret phenomena by reference to their elements or their goals, it is advisable at least to try to understand them in the sphere of experience from which they spring. Laughing and crying are forms of human expression and statement, modes of conduct, kinds of behavior. This fact brings difficulties, but also possibilities of understanding, in its wake. Theories which overlook this fact out of metaphysical or scientific prejudice are certain to go astray. Again and again, an answer to the question of why we laugh and cry has been frustrated because of such prejudices.

2. Against the Prejudice of a Dualistic Interpretation of Man, and the False Alternatives

In order to obtain a complete picture of the bodily state of a person who is laughing or crying, we would have to correlate the changes in musculature, breathing, and glandular secretion with changes in the central nervous system. This follows from the assumption that there are certain release mechanisms of the central nervous system for the characteristic forms of expression in the domain of animal as well as vegetative vital activity. If there is central regulation of breathing, body temperature, and circulation, as well as of special processes such as swallowing, blushing and turning pale, yawning, and vomiting, for example, then there is reason to suppose a central regulatory mechanism for laughing and crying. To this end, the attempt is made to evaluate specific brain diseases associated with compulsive laughing and crying.

It is not necessary to think immediately of "centers" in this connection. Laughing and crying seem rather to rest on interruptions of the normal sequence of functions than to be processes which have their "seat" (always within the limits within which it makes sense to speak of a function in general as being able to have a seat, a locus) in definite parts of the brain. Granted that physiology might have advanced so far as to arrive at clear decisions in this area, what would have been gained for the problem of laughing and crying?

An idea of the mechanism of laughing or crying, of the means of inducing these expressions: not less, but also not more.

Insight into the cooperation of the physical components of the process, however, remains unrelated to the total process of the laughing or weeping individual as long as we do not obtain from the "sense" of the total process an indication of how just these and no other physical components become effective. Why do we laugh at a joke and not weep? Why do we weep from remorse and not laugh? Even precise knowledge of the mechanism of laughing and crying cannot answer these questions. Joking and remorse may evoke a precisely localized physical excitation in the brain—there are only quite vague limits to our conjectures here—and proceeding from these specific excitations, their physical representatives, so to speak, call laughter or weeping into action. But plainly this physiological characterization of something which is nothing physical, but a system of meaning or a psychic event, is not even wishful thinking but mere nonsense.

Jokes appeal to men with a gift of reason and intellect; remorse is experienced by men with conscience and heart. It is always the *whole man* who is implicated, now more superficially, now more deeply, when he laughs or cries. The body as the seat of physiological mechanisms is not affected, and moved to react, by joking or remorse, but again only by physical "stimuli" which —if words are involved—are acoustical or optical in nature. But where reason and intellect, conscience and heart, are wanting, words, although heard or read, do not become "stimuli." In that case the configuration appropriate to release them does not arise "in the brain." Why not? Physiology knows no answer to this question; the inquiry is stuck fast in the breach between the physical and the psychical aspect.

Beyond this breach, in the domain of the internal aspect, psychology has its area of competence. Here is disclosed the understanding of joy and pain, cheerfulness and sorrow, of sensuous and intellectual feelings, emotions, moods, and thoughts. Here no limits are fixed to the analysis of complex states such as remorse and grief, commiseration and compassion, logically or aesthetically relevant contents of consciousness and combinations of ideas. But the competence of psychology ends in the area of bodily reaction. It is not in a position to comprehend the physical phenomenon of expression.

Here a typical difficulty becomes evident for the entire realm of conduct and behavior, one which is not to be overcome with our scientific resources, split as they are into physiology and psychology. As act, gesture, or mimic expression, a physical occurrence is, to be sure, stamped by the psychical and related to the physical. But this stamp and this relatedness hover, as it were, between the realm of the body, physiologically interpreted, and the realm of the mind, which is interpreted psychologically. As physical occurrences, act, gesture, and expression do not reside in the inner realm of the psychical. But if we try to lay hold of them in the play of joints and muscles, we are looking only at physical events, and their characteristic stamp is lost.

As long as science remains bound to the alternatives of the physiological versus the psychological method, the realm of behavior in the full profusion of its forms remains closed to it. In order to obtain access to this realm, we need an original method of approach to the phenomena themselves and a new confidence in everyday experience, in which we perceive our own behavior and that of others, respond to it, and come to terms with it. This confidence runs up against a crucial prejudice which constantly finds fresh sustenance from the exact natural sciences: the belief that human nature must be experienced and investigated under two fundamentally irreducible aspects because it is composed of two substances, the body (as extended thing) and the mind (as thinking thing).

This model, fashioned by Descartes, prevented the reconciliation between man as a natural thing and man as a moral and intellectual being. Physics was not to be sacrificed to the claims of theology and morality, nor theology and morality to those of physics. The strength of the model rests on this concern for two absolutely different spheres of lawfulness. Time after time, this model has prevailed against all philosophical doubts, and especially in times of rapid scientific development. Attempts have been made to soften or reinterpret its metaphysical rigor. But the dualistic conception of man has persisted, with its compulsion to separate the physical from the psychical and with its fatal possibility of playing off one against the other. Nothing in this schema is basically altered if the internal aspect in turn acquires differential avenues of access to the "psychical" and the "mental" or "intellectual," respectively. Every time, the development of scientific specialization has followed the Cartesian model. Not until the nineteenth century did the new sciences dealing with life and man—biology, sociology, and the historical disciplines dealing with culture [*die historischen Geisteswissenschaften*]—reveal the artificiality of this model and its inapplicability to experience.

The most obvious course, naturally, is to replace the ontology of Cartesianism by a monistic counterontology. This can be, and has been, done, whether on the basis of physical or mental existence or, ultimately, on the basis of a third reality, life perhaps, which then encompasses them both. Monistic constructions of this kind, frequently with reference to Spinoza, had their heyday in the nineteenth century but proved unable to influence the course of scientific development. On the contrary, the monistic principle was reduced to a hypothesis which respected the details of empirical knowledge obtained in the usual ways and sought "only" metaphysically to unify them.

Against this development, the theory of knowledge mounted its assault. Yet it was not philosophical considerations which proved decisive but the deepening and enrichment of the range of human experience, for which we are indebted to the nineteenth century. In history, ethnology, sociology, psychology, and psychopathology, men confront human beings of other times and cultures, with other attitudes toward life and other forms of self-interpretation. The obviousness of one's own familiar existence itself becomes questionable, and its interpretation, followed and acknowledged as valid for centuries, loses its persuasive power. In consequence, old models of human nature lost their value, but the readiness to replace them by new ones was weakened by relativism.

Out of this characteristic attitude of our time, a time marked by the lack of confidence in reason, another type of opposition to Cartesianism has arisen, which differs from the monistic. This new opposition wishes, not simply to replace the dualistic model of human nature by another, but to render it superfluous. It does not take up the mind-body problem at all, but attempts to do away with it as an artificial difficulty, an unnecessary construction, a misconception. In truth, this attitude evades the problem by going back to an allegedly unproblematic, primordial level of existence, which coincides with the level of conduct or behavior in its *niveau* but not in its inner structure. By a technique which, as we shall point out in greater detail, is always feasible, the forms of behavior are so characterized from the start that the cleft between "inner" and "outer" does not appear at all. In this way, the semblance of a primordial problem-free human condition is produced—at any rate, with regard to the relation of the psyche, i.e., man, to the body.

In the face of such irresponsibility and carelessness in the treatment of nature, which marks the fashionable anti-Cartesianism, phenomena like laughing and crying force us to show our true colors and stand up for the real difficulty of human existence. Speaking, acting, shaping, and expressive movement do not of themselves necessitate this.[5] In these instances, the human body accommodates itself to impulses and intentions of a psychological nature. The body goes along with, allows itself to be molded by, sustains, and, just because it is so tractable, also demands no other role than that of matter, embodying stuff, the compliant means of presentation. As stuff and medium, it means that from which intelligible content can emancipate itself. This aspect fits the interpretation of man which has become traditional under the dominance of the dualistic schema: the body is the enveloping layer, indispensable to life and unavoidable for the purpose of expression, of a being which in its true nature knows itself to be emancipated from this envelope and has command over it to the limits of sickness and death.

Laughing and crying provide another view of the relation of man to his body. Their form of utterance, whether expressive or expressionless, whether full or empty of meaning, reveals as such no symbolic form. Although initially motivated by us, laughing and crying make their appearance as uncontrolled and unformed eruptions of the body, which acts, as it were, autonomously. Man falls into their power; he breaks—out laughing, and lets himself break—into tears. He responds to something by laughing and crying, but not with a form of expression which could be appropriately compared with verbal utterance, expressive movement, gesture, or action. He responds—with his body as body, as if from the impossibility of being able to find an answer himself. And in the loss of control over himself and his body, he reveals himself at the same time as a more than bodily being who lives in a state of tension with regard to his physical existence yet is wholly and completely bound to it.

From this impenetrability in the relation of man to his body, earlier analysis has recoiled. Even where it rose above the prejudices of a dualistic psychophysics (for example, in the direction influenced by Klages, as well as in many existential psychologists and pathologists) it was limited to the sphere of the rationally significant, to symbolically formed kinds of behavior, i.e., to actions, expressive movements, and gestures. Such analyses emphasized on principle the cooperation and interaction of the psychical and the physical from the point of view of their greatest possible convergence, indeed, their unity. Whatever disturbs this image, or at any rate does not immediately fit in with it, whatever, in its motoric and static aspects, is not derivable from motivational theory, was put aside, and turned over to a physiology presumably competent to deal with it.

It was overlooked that man has, not a univocal, but an equivocal relation to his body, that his existence imposes on him the ambiguity of being an "embodied" [*leibhaften*] creature and a creature "in the body" [*im Körper*], an ambiguity that means an actual break in his way of existing. It is this brokenness that distinguishes what phenomena like laughter and tears suggest: the impenetrability of man's relation to his body.

It will be the task of the following study to show that man's ambiguous position as living body in a physical body [*Leib im Körper*] constitutes the basis of laughing and crying—a position which is also present in his other monopolies, like speech, expressive movement, the use of clothing and tools. To this end, the inquiry must free itself from the bias inherent in the Cartesian interpretation of human existence. The two-substance theory, which survives as a double-aspect theory, in the rigid and seemingly self-evident alternative: physical or mental, is not capable of understanding the phenomena of laughing and crying. Hence it would be a crude misunderstanding to reduce the "ambiguity" of physical existence to a duality of interpretation, that is, to consciousness. The brokenness of man's relation to his body is rather the basis of his existence, the source, but also the limit, of his power.

3. The Eccentric Position

Beginning with man in the original concreteness of his existence, laughing and crying are to be comprehended as physical reactions. In the appended phrase "as physical reactions," however, we are not expressing any abandonment of understanding from the unitary perspective of man as a being who rejoices and sorrows and with heart and mind is bound to a whole world. On the other hand, with respect to physiology, the limits of its competence have convinced us that the problem can no more be left to this science than to psychology or the double-aspect science of psychophysics. With the phrase "as physical reactions," we only mean to emphasize that this study does not recoil from the genuine difficulty of understanding bodily events, as is elsewhere the practice of philosophy, because it allegedly has nothing to do with them. The cleverly chosen perspective of existential analysis bypasses the true problems of human existence and consequently a real knowledge of it.

Compared with speech, gesture, and mimic expressive movements, laughing and crying attest to an incalculable emancipation of bodily events from the person. In this disproportion and willfulness, we surmise, lies what is truly revelatory in the phenomena. In no other form of expression is the secret composition of human nature more directly disclosed than in these.

Speaking and acting show man in his mastery at the height of the free power of control given to him through reason. If he loses mastery here, he sinks below his proper level. To be sure, this sinking testifies to the height originally occupied, but it does not disclose the way in which man is bound to his body.

We learn just as little of this type of bond when a man loses control over himself in cases of the narrowing, clouding, or blacking-out of his consciousness, as through overpowering emotion or the use of narcotics. For in such cases the human unity of the person is destroyed.

And finally, nothing of this bond is revealed by partially reflexive reactions such as blushing, turning pale, sweating, vomiting, coughing, and sneezing—all dependent for their identity on a more or less artificial separation. For these reactions can indeed be psychologically induced in situations involving shame, anxiety, terror, repugnance, and disgust—embarrassment and excitement generally. But they lack the character of being conscious responses. Their symbolism—to which psychoanalytically oriented medicine pays even more attention today than thirty years ago—is not something for which the subject directly knows himself to be responsible. As in cases of psychosomatic illness, the process here reflects only symptomatically a disturbance of personal existence.

On the other hand, with laughing and crying the person does indeed lose control, but he remains a person, while the body, so to speak, takes over the answer for him. With this is disclosed a possibility of cooperation between the person and his body, a possibility which usually remains hidden because it is not usually invoked.

Usually, in unequivocal situations which can be unequivocally answered and controlled, man responds *as* a person and makes use of his body for that pupose: as an instrument of speech, as a grasping, thrusting, supporting, and conveying organ, as a means of locomotion, as a means of signaling, as the sounding board of his emotions. He controls his body, or learns to control it.

This control, individually fluctuating, is subject to certain limits, probably not rigid, and which certainly do not coincide with the boundaries between voluntary and involuntary regulation. Nor is the distribution of nervous processes among the partly consciously, partly unconsciously operative system of animal functions (the sensorimotor system) and the unconsciously operative system of vegetative functions (which regulates the processes of circulation, metabolism, and internal secretion and is important for the *milieu interne* and for internal equilibrium, for mood and emotional state) decisive in determining the extent of man's control over his body.

(If certain reports are to be believed, many people can exercise control over circulation, breathing, and even the regulation of body temperature. The autonomic processes—and anyone who practices a bit of training in will power can convince himself of this—are in any event more susceptible to influence by the total human attitude than present-day physiology generally assumes, since it has civilized man in view. Training in the field of sport is wholly oriented toward the sensorimotor, animal system. While it does indeed master many autonomic processes, it intervenes from without and does not follow the path of the classical techniques of self-control through self-submergence.)

The goal of mastery—either in the service of the affirmation of man's bodily existence, in which case it is oriented now to maximum performance, now to complete relaxation, i.e., grace, or in the service of the denial of the body, i.e., asceticism and escape—is set to man by his physical existence: lived body *in* a physical body [*als* Leib *im* Körper]. From the day of his birth on, everyone must come to terms with this double role. Every kind of learning, e.g., grasping and the correlation of its effects with visual distance, standing, running, and so on, takes place on the basis and within the framework of this double role. The frame itself is never broken. A human being always and conjointly *is* a living body (head, trunk, extremities, with all that these contain)—even if he is convinced of his immortal soul, which somehow exists "therein"—and *has* this living body as this physical thing.

The possibility of using such different verbal expressions to refer to physical existence is rooted in the ambiguous character of this existence itself. A man has it, and he is it. He confronts his physical existence as something which he masters or sets aside, something which he uses as a means, an instrument; he is in it *and* (to a given extent) coincides with it. Thus bodily existence for man is a *relation,* in itself not unequivocal, but ambiguous, a relation of himself to himself [*sich . . . sich*] (or, to put it precisely, of him to himself). *Who* it is that stands in this relation can remain open. Nor do verbal expressions like "mind," "I," "soul"—if we take them without a dogmatic religious sense —say more than everyday social experience convincingly reveals of our confrontation with the body and yet inclusion by it.

Convincingly and fundamentally, because our behavior toward the environment, both in its practical execution and in its interpretation by our fellow man, is shaped by this double role. Since it is usually taken for granted, only a reflective person can take cognizance of it as such. For we have come to terms with our double role, even theoretically, in such a fashion as to conjure away its immediacy.

Everyone speaks of his "I," his "self," whose domain extends in each case no further than the confining surfaces of his own body, but yet, as nonspatial, stands in its turn over against this domain. It asserts itself within, now in the region of the breast as the subject of sympathy, feeling, and desire, now in the region of the head as the subject of reflection, observation, and attention. "Within," at the level of breast or head, and "inside one's own body" are again descriptions which, though contradicting the nonspatial nature of the self, nevertheless persist and appeal to everyone's self-experience. We can enhance this paradoxical insight by thought experiments, but we cannot overcome it: behind eyes and ears, *I* sit as the center of my consciousness; between breast and back live disposition and "heart." My thoughts and desires, hidden to others, seem, lying within and surrounded by the body, to belong to a spaceless deep.

This internal location of myself in my body is enmeshed, in a way entirely obvious to common sense, in an immediate location of myself within the space of things. Here I am separated from the "outer" world, not by an intermediate layer, which I, as a separate entity, live through and "comprehend" from within, but as myself a piece of the external world, somewhere in a room or on the street. Here stands my body *qua* content of my visual or tactile field, of my locomotor, attentional, and visceral sensations, on the same line with other physical things which appear within the horizon of my perception. Regardless of whether I move about and do something or quietly let the images of the external world, including my own body as a part of it, act on me, the situation of my existence is ambiguous: *as* physical lived body—*in* the physical lived body.

Both orders [6] are entwined in each other and form a remarkable unity. Each can indeed be observed and characterized in itself, but they cannot be separated. I go walking *with* my consciousness, my body is its bearer, on whose momentary position the selective content and perspective of my consciousness depend; and I go walking *in* my consciousness, and my own body with its changes of position appears as the content of its sphere.

To wish to make a decision between these two orders would mean to misunderstand the necessity of their mutual interlacing. But with the same justification, I must hold firm to two mutually exclusive orders; that is, I must insist on the absolute focal reference of all things in the environment to my body, or to the center of perception, thinking, initiative, and sympathy persisting "in" it, i.e., to me or the "self" in me; *and* I must give up this absolute focal reference in favor of the relative localization of all things, including my body (together with my consciousness). Both orders are evident in the dual role of man as body and in the body. Both suggest powerful motives and arguments for the idealistic as well as the realistic theories of consciousness or nature, theories whose polemics can no more easily be settled than prevented, since the situation to which they appeal is necessarily ambiguous.

In this situation, the human position can be understood as *eccentric*. Just as the world and my own body are revealed to me, and can be controlled by me, only insofar as they appear in relation to me as a central "I," so, on the other hand, they retain their ascendancy over their subjection in this perspective as an order indifferent to me and including me in a nexus of mutual neighborhoods.

Even if man can come to no decision between these two orders, the one related to a center and the other not, he must nevertheless find a relation to them. For he is totally merged in neither. Neither *is* he just living body, nor does he just *have* a body. Every requirement of physical existence demands a reconciliation between being and having, outside and inside.

In the normal course of life, with its attachment to accustomed goals, this pressure for reconciliation is not conspicuous. In unusual situations, on the other hand, it meets with difficulties. These may involve questions of spatial orientation, of the estimation of size and distance in the perceptual field, or of the coordination of bodily movements with external things and with one's own body. Everyone knows from his own experience how easy it is to become confused in matters involving symmetry, mirror images, and the relations of left and right. Moreover, in recent times, clinical experiments in the areas of aphasia, ataxia, and apraxia have brought to light a wealth of material on disturbances to which the relation of man to his body can be subject. Among the basic insights which we owe to these studies is precisely the knowledge that it is here a question of the relation to the body or, more accurately, of the reconciliation between being a body and having a body in particular situations, and not merely a question of deficiencies occasioned by disturbances of the nervous system.

Moreover, we need only demand of our body some unaccustomed activity to find ourselves again faced with problems like those of a child learning to walk. The pressure for reconciliation between the two kinds of physical existence then presents itself, for example, as a problem of balance or of weight distribution. Thus expressions like "he has to have it in his bones" mean, not simply that a movement consciously brought about and controlled must become a reflex, but that the reconciliation between having a body and being one must take place readily and quickly. Each individual must come to terms with this in his own way—and in a certain sense can never come to terms with it.

In this respect man is inferior to the animal since the animal does not experience itself as shut off from its physical existence, as an inner self or I, and in consequence does not have to overcome a break between itself and itself, itself and its physical existence. The fact of an animal's being a body does not cut it off from its having one. It does indeed live in this separation—no movement, no leap (which an appraisal of distance must precede) would be possible without it. The animal too must put its body into action, employ it according to the given situation;

otherwise, it does not reach its goal. But the switch from being to having, from having to being, which the animal constantly performs, does not in its turn present itself to him, nor, consequently, does it present any difficulty to him.[7]

The lack of inhibition which makes the animal superior to man in control determines at the same time its restriction to the role that happens to be biologically assigned to it. It cannot come upon the idea (nor, in general, on any idea) to try out with its body something not immediately prescribed by its motor functions and instincts. Things may go ever so well with real donkeys; yet they never venture out on the ice.*

Only man is impersonally *and* personally aware of his physical situation, a constant restraint but also a constant incentive to overcome it. From the first, man's relation to himself as living body has an instrumental character, because he experiences his body as "means." In the compulsion ever again to find a new accommodation between the physical thing which he somehow happens to be and the body which he inhabits and controls—and not only by artificial abstraction—man comes to discover the mediated character, the instrumental character, of his concrete physical existence.

4. Mediateness and Explicitness. Face and Voice

It would seem that our last observations on man's special position, his specific mode of being, have taken us away from our theme. In reality, they provide the foundation for its discussion. If laughing and crying are human monopolies, then they must be understood through human nature. For this purpose, the usual characterization through concepts like soul and mind is insufficient. Apart from the ambiguity and incomprehensibility which cling to them because of their theological and metaphysical past, these concepts leave us in the lurch in questions of the relation to the body. If it is objected to our observations that they convey nothing which could not be understood through the nature of man as a person, distinguished by selfhood [*Ichhaftigkeit*] and rationality [*Geistigkeit*], such an objection misunderstands what they have been attempting. They seek, from the first, to secure the determination of man's physical

* From the proverb: *Wenn dem Esel zu wohl wird, geht er aufs Eis:* "The overconfident jackass tries to skate." Its counterpart in English is "Pride goeth before a fall."—J. S. C.

existence and within its horizon to outline the specific character of human life as "being-there" [*Da-sein*].

On this account, we have deliberately chosen to introduce a neutral concept like that of "eccentric position," which refrains from every interpretation of what is essentially human and authentic. In conscious avoidance of loaded, ambiguous words, which conceal the intuitively obvious, basic facts, this concept points to those facts as the constitution and manner of embodied human existence. It also preserves neutrality of aspect against the temptation to espouse now the external, now the internal side of the dualistic model of man: the temptation to determine the constitution of human existence according to physical or psychological categories and then afterwards, in order to make up for the damage of this one-sidedness, to arrange a compromise between outer and inner. To the shift of viewpoint to which, incipiently, all living existence, but in its full development only human existence, compels us, the concept of "eccentricity" is, not indifferent, but neutral. As the formal designation of a "standing in . . . ," it encompasses the double aspect of outer and inner and thus makes possible the differentiated apprehension of the human relation to one's own body.

If, in this concept, we have caught the human manner of embodied being in the world, then it must be possible to develop from it those essential characteristics which are specifically human, such as speech, the use of tools, dress, religiosity, social organization, the development of power, art: in short, the regions of expression and representation peculiar to man. As necessary possibilities, which a being of eccentric position can have at its command, they can be reduced in a number of respects.

In my *Stufen des Organischen und der Mensch,* which introduced the concept of eccentric position and substantiated it by a theory of organic categories, I summarized these necessary possibilities from a threefold point of view: from the standpoint of the natural-artificial, the immediate-mediated, and the rooted-groundless. The basic anthropological laws of natural artificiality, mediated immediacy, and utopian standpoint thus mediate between the fundamental constitution of the eccentric position and the typical modes of human activity. They are linked to the historically attested interpretation of human being without claiming to exhaust all the possibilities implicit in it. The points of view under which these laws are summarized are not presented as the only ones conceivable, although they were not chosen arbitrarily but with a view to the great areas of human production.

Eccentric position makes possible in like manner, for example, the gift of speech and the need for clothing (thus, conceptualization and the consciousness of nakedness); or upright posture and religious consciousness; or the use of tools and interest in decoration. Physical and mental "properties," in which man shows himself to be man, as tendencies, capacities, abilities, or however we wish to designate the modes of self-interpretation and presentation of human existence: all these are grounded equally radically in this concept.

To be sure, we should not conceive of this foundation as a single source from which everything springs, as if all possible properties put in their appearance from a single basic constitution. For these specifically human gifts are connected most intimately together and have need of one another, or at least evoke one another. For example, since standing upright freed the hands for grasping, the use of tools and an upright gait form a unity, quite apart from the other advantages that resulted from the achievement of upright posture: advantages for the extension of the perceptual field, the emancipation from the immediate environment, the development of the cerebrum—and with the latter, again, the differentiation of intelligence—or, in another direction, for the understanding of one's own body as an instrument and thus the gift of speech.

In the eccentric position, the formal condition is given under which man's essential characteristics and monopolies appear in their indissoluble unity (indissoluble in meaning), quite apart from the question, to what aspect of human existence they are ascribed, whether to the physical, psychic, or mental. Consequently, provided that they belong among the human monopolies, laughing and crying must likewise be intelligible, along with the other essential characters, under the formal condition of the eccentric position.

The problem will be to hit upon the right spot in the web of reciprocal connections. As forms of expression adjacent to speech and mime, laughing and crying belong to the sphere of expressivity. It will become evident that this sphere is closely connected with the situation of imprisonment in one's own body which we have already outlined. Thus the analysis takes up the thread of the discussion again and begins with what was last said about the instrumental, or means, character of the body.

Only to man, so we said, is his situation as body given at once impersonally and personally. He experiences himself *as* a thing and *in* a thing: but a thing which differs absolutely from all other things because he himself is that thing, because it obeys his intentions or at least responds to them. He is borne by it, encompassed by it, developed to effectiveness with and by it, yet at the same time it forms a resistance never to be wholly overcome. In this unity, of the relation to his physical existence as impersonally and personally given, a unity which he must constantly renew, man's living body is disclosed to him as a means, i.e., as something he can utilize to move about, carry loads, sit, lie, grasp, strike, and so on. This adaptability, together with its independent, objective thinghood, makes the living body an instrument.

The same also holds true of animals, but with the limitation that they achieve this instrumentality without being aware of it and without first having to find a relation to it. In the singular withdrawal [*Abgehobenheit*] from his physical existence which makes it possible for man to say "I" to himself, his situation in the world is presented to him as a *mediated* immediacy. By means of my body, I am in immediate contact, experienced as immediate, with the things in my environment. Seeing, hearing, touching, every sensation, visualization, and perception, has the import of being fulfilled in an immediate presentation of the colors and shapes, the sounds, surface configurations, and solidity of the things themselves. Granted, consideration of the fact that intervening processes in the sense organs, nerves, and central nervous system are necessary for such presentation complicates the substantiation of this truth, but it does not nullify it. The image of the object on the retina is admittedly inverted, but "I" do not need to reinvert it in my head in order that the correct impression, as I really have it, should occur. For I do not see the retinal image, and my brain does not see it either. The latter is a piece of protoplasm, which cannot see.

Such facts, among which one must also reckon the sense-specific energies of the nerves themselves, give rise, understandably, to the basic mistrust of the objectivity and inherent accuracy of our sensations and perceptions. First the secondary qualities of sense and then even the primary qualities were subjectivized, and the further development of subjective idealism went so far as to absorb completely even the ultimate describability and self-presence of the real in consciousness. Consciousness itself remained as a mere conjuror's stage and so lost all significance. With the one-sided exaggeration of the mediating and mediated aspect, its immediacy, the contact of I and world in knowing and acting, was bound to perish.

It makes no sense to oppose the fact of mediated immediacy and to keep trying to put simpler models in its place, be they models of immanence or of transcendence, of closure from or openness to what there is [*das Seiende*]. Those times of epistemology should be over. Only in the entwining of withdrawal and presence, remoteness and proximity, does the immanence of consciousness fulfill its function of disclosing reality. Only in the mediation by my body, which I myself bodily am (although I also possess it), is the I with things, looking and acting. As in all analysis, the demonstrable existence of connecting links such as chemical processes, contents of consciousness, images, and psychical processes interrupts, for our conception of it, the significance of this very mediation, just as an isolated presentation of individual notes cancels out their musical significance. In the course of the mediation, on the other hand, their significance is realized: to cancel one another in order to produce an immediate relation between the terms related.

Mediated immediacy is just as little to be "explained" as other "lower" modes of living. It is itself a basis for the explanation of the role of spatial, material processes in the structure of consciousness, for example, of its illusions and their corrections. If we take mediated immediacy as basic, then we can get further in questions pertaining to brain and mind, consciousness and object, than was possible up to now under the guidance of worn-out theories involving bisubstantial, double-aspect, two-component models.

Within the framework of mediated immediacy, i.e., of the eccentric position, as presented in terms of the relation of I and body, problems can be stated with greater precision and lead to a future solution, where within the old framework, with its crude alternatives, we at once struck the boundaries of all knowledge. As a mode of life, the eccentric position is reducible to, and so intelligible in terms of, certain laws of structure governing all living things—and that not only more or less, but exactly. But it is not to be explained in terms, say, of matter. Certain elemental and radical modes of being must be accepted, among them life and its positional character, i.e., its modes of relation to the environment. One of these is the eccentric position of man, with the perplexities and monopolies, infirmities and strengths, that belong to it specifically.

We have already argued that the possibility, particularly reserved to man, of controlling nature objectively in knowing and doing, is rooted in mediated immediacy. Indeed, in terms of the problems arising from the immanence of consciousness, i.e., from the standpoint of cognition alone, this insight has long been familiar to us. Corresponding to this character is the *instrumentality* of the body, which, however, again emphasizes only one side of the relation to physical existence (but an important one, since to a substantial degree the use of tools, inventive intelligence, and *Homo faber* are anchored in it).

A no less important side of this relation is the *expressivity* of the body, which manifests itself in very diverse ways in gesture, mime, posture, speech, and naturally also in forms of expression like laughing and crying. But its nature is not exhausted in any of its characteristic forms. Nor do phrases like "drive to expression," "tendency toward vocal expression" (or even "communication") render it without distortion. Expression is a fundamental trait of mediated immediacy and, like the instrumentality of the body or the objectivity of knowledge, corresponds to that tension and entwinement which we are always having to adjust, between being a body and having a body. Expressivity is a fundamental way of coming to terms with the fact that man occupies a body and yet is a body.

Again, this also holds true for animals—with the restriction that they achieve expressivity without being aware of it and without having to find a position to take to it. They live in it, and hence their body mirrors the change of excitation in typical expressive movements (change of color, ruffling of feathers, erection of crest, sound) but with complete absence of gesture, speech, or laughing and crying. In expressive movement and posture, the "inner" becomes visible, it moves outward. This externalization occurs on the animal level as the direct radiation from the center of excitation to the periphery of the bodily surfaces. To the extent that man also lives on the animal level—and the eccentric position includes the centric position of the animal, by encircling it—he deports himself expressively in ways not basically different from animals. Many expressive gestures in the spheres of mime and sound are common to men and animals. Greed, fear, terror, surprise, pleasure, depression, joy, restlessness and repose, rage, hesitation, watchfulness, and many other kinds of dispositional states in the behavior linked to vital sources show the same dynamic morphology in animal and man.

For the creature gripped by excitement, expression, as the outward movement and shaping of the "internal," takes place immediately on the level of expressive movement. But that this can occur bears witness to a relation of inner and outer that is ambiguous, since inner and outer are reciprocally interrelated. In animals, too, the body as expressive surface is no passive envelope and external layer into which excitations boil over from within, but a felt boundary surface over against the environment. Although external, it belongs from the very first with the internal. Animals live this relation, and—to the extent that he exists on this level—so does man. But only he knows of it.

This "knowing of it" is no occasional act of reflection which leaves the expressive relation untouched, taking place only beyond and apart from it. It is a luminosity and a distance into which our own expressive life is displaced. In this way, it can become the basis of an autonomous expressive system (in gesture and speech). Apart from this, however, body surface and voice, the natural sounding boards of expression, acquire throughout the character of being "organs of expression." Thus, expressivity is set free to become a power more or less at the disposal of the individual, which permits the individual, under certain conditions, to assume an artificial mask and posture, as the actor shows. That man must constantly take this power into account in order to find a balanced relation to his physical existence, he learns at every hand; for it is difficult to remain natural, to speak and behave spontaneously. Everyone is predisposed (and needs) to assume the attitude of his social position, his home, his calling, and his ideal. Naturalness is a task which appears to man in many guises when, in his personal or social development, he penetrates the artificiality of his existence.

Body surface and voice, the primal sounding boards of expression, have for the power or "faculty" of expressivity the character of organs of expression. That is, they appear as means and fields of expression, with and in which it becomes externally perceptible. In this process, that part of the body which is naturally outside the range of self-perception, i.e., the *face,* takes the lead and (with certain limits) becomes its representative. As the posture of the whole body mirrors in itself the mental state, so the face—and, again in a concentrated way, the look—becomes the mirror, indeed the "window," of the soul. As the area of sight and vocal utterance, a man's face is at once imperceptible and open. He looks out of and sounds forth from it, and by means of it captures the glances of others, the vistas of the world. Concealment and overtness make the face the front, the boundary and mediating surface of one's own against the other, the inner against the outer. So, even on the animal level, the outer is no mere containing wall which encloses something inner, but it is incorporated into the inner and, conversely, implicates the inner—becoming a true boundary through the autonomy of this double outer-inner relation. This relation not only expresses and subsists on a "reciprocity of perspectives"; it *gives expression to* them. Thus eyes, mouth, and nose as such do not make up the face, for, if this were true, animals too would have faces. Only the eccentric position toward the world gives these features this sense of unity, to the deployment of which the upright posture, the development of forehead, chin, and nose, and the free mobility of the head contribute, each in its way.

Like the face with its unmistakable cast of features, the *voice* is also a primal sounding board for expression—for man: his organ. In and with his voice, man stretches out and lays hold on the other, as he himself is attuned and held. If concealment from oneself and overtness toward the world are characteristic of the face, so that through his face the individual is completely exposed and delivered over to every counterreaction before he can protect himself by facial mime, the voice is the ideal medium of deployment from the internal to the external. It can be graduated according to strength, pitch, and emotional and persuasive force; it can be modulated and articulated, whether as sung or spoken sound, as "bearer" of musical or linguistic communication.

The self-control and self-transparency of the voice supplement the frontal openness to the outside, the inner concealment, through which, in two directions, but without gradual transition, the face confronts men with one another and with the world, as observing-observable. In it we step, constantly hearing ourselves, open and exposed from within as well as without, in a gradual transition of regulable deployment into the communal system of informing and being informed.[8]

This also holds—within the limits mentioned above—for the air-breathing animals. Inhaling and exhaling govern the possibilities of giving voice and serve as the basis for the many species-specific sounds of warning and enticement which accompany the biologically important situations as signals or purely expressive attitudes. They guarantee a contact which occasionally evokes the appearance of speech and mutual understanding, or even of song (as with birds), although (and this is also true of anthropoid apes) they never lose their vital connection and in no wise achieve autonomy from emotion. Animals "give cry," and the wealth of their vocalizations reveals many kinships with the vocalizations of man. Shrieking and moaning, groaning and sighing, jabbering and yowling: molds evoked under strong internal pressure, by pain, confinement, frustration, fatigue, already appear among the higher vertebrates. Less frequent are sounds indicative of ease, of pleasure, in states of satiation and relaxation; more frequent, on the other hand, are sounds of delight, of physical surprise, of aggressiveness, in which the internal pressure increases with such force as to relieve itself.

Such sudden release also marks the vital-functional side of the higher forms of expression reserved to man, such as gesture, speech, and laughing and crying, especially at times when, as in the last case, strong emotion and tension compel their discharge. The repression of an excitation, which is manifested in an appropriately sudden breakdown, we find widely distributed in the animal world. In order that such repression may be relieved through laughing and crying, both occasion and possibilities of release must be given, which only man, in his eccentric position toward the world and his own physical existence, has at his disposal. The specific occasions we will treat separately. On the other hand, the possibilities of release can be correctly understood only against the background of these forms of expression as a whole. In everyday life, the human modes of expression constantly overlap one another, supplement one another, and have grown so close together that speech, gesture, mime, and facial expressive movement cannot be sharply recognized in themselves. Nevertheless, such a characterization of the modes of expression is the only way to arrive at a clear demarcation of the unique nature of laughing and crying.

The uncertainty of the situation in this respect is revealed by the mere fact that in professional treatment the theme of laughing far outweighs that of crying. So pronounced is this ascendancy that we must ask ourselves seriously whether, in general, laughing and crying really form a pair of expressions and present a true contrast in the way that people generally believe. Our analysis of these modes of human expression will always keep in mind the question of their coordinate relationship.

2 / The Modes of Expression of Laughing and Crying

Do WE FIND REFLECTED in the contrast between laughing and crying only the dualism of joy and sorrow, pleasure and pain, according to which we usually classify our relations to the world? Usually, the stresses are divided according to this dualism: we laugh for joy and cry for sorrow. The beaming countenance, the unfurrowed brow, the sparkling eyes, the open mouth with its corners drawn upward, the well-rounded cheeks, the play of light and the crinkles about the eyes and nose, the rippling volley of unmanageable sound: all are the reflection of a radiant, unburdened world. In the veiled, slackened countenance of the weeper with his streaming, unseeing eyes, the turned-down corners of the mouth, the furrowed brow, in his incessant, jerky sobbing, sighing, and whimpering we see depicted a darkened world under the weight of an oppressive burden. The contrast between the expressive images seems to correspond in the most obvious way to the contrast of feeling. Elation and mobility on the one hand, oppression and lassitude on the other.

But is it really so simple? Thanks to our tendency to paint everything black or white and to group things according to good and evil, true and false, beautiful and ugly, pleasing and offensive, are we not tempted to correlate the contrast of laughing and crying with that of pleasure and displeasure?

On the side of laughter, the supposition may seem at first sight to be quite plausible. For whatever the source of a person's good spirits in a particular case—a happy surprise, a funny sight, a joke, even gallows humor or self-irony—it is always a kind of escape and elevation which manifests itself in laughter. On the side of crying, however, things are more complicated.

Here what varies is not only the sources of suffering and sorrow but the emotional state itself which is discharged in crying. We may discern in sadness the character of suffering and also associate repentance with suffering, sorrow, and grief. But whence come the tears of unexpected good fortune, love, bliss, deliverance, conversion, devotion, transport, and exaltation? Why do we cry in the grip of strong emotion, in ecstasy? What moves a person to tears at the peak of fulfillment, now that every pressure, everything dark, painful, or depressing, has given way and the boundlessness of a new life opens up before him?

Even these first hints reveal the impossibility of correlating the contrast of laughing and crying with that of pleasure and pain and of making the simple schema of "up" and "down" the basis of their strange opposition. But how else to grasp this contrast? The variety of sources of weeping, its incomparable emotional depth as opposed to laughter, could bring this opposition itself into question; it could result in assigning their respective manifestations to different levels of personal life. But the manner of their expression allows us to discern a kinship which confirms their opposition. Their foundation must admittedly be sought elsewhere than in the usual direction.

1. Language, Gesture, and Expressive Movement

Macroscopically, human expression is exhibited in two realms: language and expressive movement.

Language makes use of articulated sounds as signs of meanings which can express an actual state of affairs without being linked to either the emotional state or the situation of the speaker. It is not the speaker as such but the language he speaks that communicates, and the path of communication runs, not as in an understanding glance, in the play of mutual excitement and of affective resonance, from person to person, but indirectly, via the intended content of the statement. Speaking is a matter of expressing, communicating, and combining through the medium of saying *something.** Evidently, only man has this possibility at his disposal. The "antenna language" of ants, the enticing and warning sounds typical of many animal species (especially gregarious types), the twittering of birds, even the typical emotional cries of apes and monkeys are forms of signaling, of expression, of communication and association in the

* *des Sagens auf dem Grunde einer Sache.*

form of direct contact from individual to individual. They lack the medium of "saying some*thing*."

The sentimental confusion with which the animal-lover tries to blur this distance between man and animal through his defense of true animal language receives fresh support time and again from the existence of *gesticulatory language, of gesture,* in man. Words are lacking in this language; the body alone speaks, and that it speaks is attested, not only by the success of mutual understanding, but also by the representative nature of the gestures. It is precisely this representative character which should serve as a warning to the animal-lover, as well as to the evolutionary biologist, not to see in gesticulatory language a connecting link between animal and human language, between expressive movement and talk. Tail-wagging is an expressive movement of the dog and not a gesture, like, for example, shrugging the shoulders or shaking the head in man. When we wink, or wrinkle our nose, or make a motion with our hand, we convey information to someone in a definite situation, because among men, especially among men belonging to the same tradition, we may presuppose that they understand such signs as substitutes for whole sentences and grasp the intended meaning in its objective context, even without words. But where, as with the animal, the possibility of understanding and apprehending meaning as meaning, i.e., on the basis of objective facts, is wholly excluded, there can be no gestures which can function allegorically and metaphorically to say much, or everything, in place of words.

There remains only the question, which is difficult and certainly not to be decided in general terms, of the extent of agreement in the origin of particular movements. We know that even the signs for affirmation and denial are not common to all peoples. We know, for example, that in many societies the gesture of nose-rubbing corresponds to that of kissing; that many are not familiar with the use of the handclasp in greeting and departure; that raising the right hand can take the place of lifting the hat. Nevertheless, there is a mimic, an emotional and expressive element, concealed in every gesture. This is true not only in the sense that its constant use allows the conventional element to be forgotten, with the result that it is taken for granted as a "natural" expressive movement. On the contrary, the convention behind the actual gesture must go back to a natural movement, must have had an expressive and mimic point of contact, in order to be able to utilize this movement. The repertoire of gesticulatory language *stylizes* an expressive content. For this reason, it does not remain mere mime but becomes language, the symbols of which are gestures, i.e., bodily expressive movements (in some circumstances also spontaneous vocal utterances *).

The existence of a gesticulatory language, which only man has at his disposal, because only he and not the animal can speak, does not do away with the division of expressional activity into language and mime. Such a language is no transitional structure between the two forms of expression even if it does give expression to linguistic sign function in unspoken material. It is a kind of language and, if necessary, for example with the deaf and dumb, capable of considerable discrimination. To be sure, gesticulatory language does not make use of articulated sound complexes as vehicles of meaning but of bodily, and occasionally also acoustical, movements; but by means of such movements it conveys information and, indeed, in a manner analogous to speech, since it invests them with a symbolic character. This wordless speech often takes the place of spoken words. (Gestures of command, pointing, attestation, entreaty, submission, gestures indicating "perhaps," "yes," "no," "thanks," "delighted," etc., play an important role in social intercourse.) And, occasionally, such gestures serve to weaken or strengthen verbal discourse. In every case they have a meaning which they convey through signs and thereby qualify as language, not as mime.

But why this detailed discussion? Because there is a recent tendency to give laughter (and occasionally crying also) the character of gesticulatory language. The special position of laughter among the forms of expressive movement, its restriction to man, its strong connection with community life, which in turn gives it a social function—all these factors seem to many theorists best accounted for by explaining laughter as a kind of speech or instinctive gesture. Three things may be brought against this view: the universal distribution of laughing and crying among all peoples and at all periods; their compulsive onset and discharge in certain situations; and, finally, their character as purely expressive and reactive, the lack of sign function present to the consciousness of the laughing or crying individual.

* E.g., cries and groans.—M. G.

Where these factors are present, we cannot, in a strict sense, talk of language, not even of gesticulatory language. The honorific use of the word "language" in a figurative sense by critics and historians of art (in phrases like "the tonal language of Beethoven," "the emotional language of Bernini," or "the sovereign language of Rembrandt's brushstrokes") has contributed to the conceptual confusion in this area no less than the sentimental mixup, already mentioned, of the animal-lover who misunderstands himself and his charges when he promotes their expressive movements to gestures.

Expressive movements as such are immediate, spontaneous, and intrinsically unrelated to others, i.e., are without intentional character, even when the presence of others is necessary for the release of the expression. To the extent that the body is covered by clothing, expressive movements are concentrated essentially in the face, although in many cases there is also a sympathetic involvement of the rest of the body. Hence it would be mistaken to look upon the posture and expressive bearing of the whole body as separate from facial expression. Joy and rage, dread and courage, grief and horror, exuberance and sloth, express themselves pantomimically in the whole body, even though the finer play of the facial muscles around the mouth and eyes permits us to follow the development and variation of the expression in its more delicate nuances. Envy, shame, remorse, and eagerness are perhaps limited to this area of expression and make the face the true reflective surface, the sounding board of psychic excitation, just as turning pale and blushing also make their appearance especially in the face. But even laughing and crying are not restricted to the face.

(That the prevalence of definite emotional states stamps a person's features in the course of his development, no one can deny. The only question is, to what extent. Any popular study of physiognomy certainly makes the matter seem too simple. Surely a sensuous, pleasure-loving mouth belongs to a different level of interpretation from the "pointed chin of the miser" or the "typical musician's head." The formative power of an occupation, of a psychological or intellectual predisposition, of an inclination or temperament, must certainly be distinguished from the mysterious fitness of a certain physical build for a definite "character" [or form of personality]. Here the interpretation is subject to the greatest possible variety of errors. If a so-called property of the psyche can be the resultant of the most diverse circumstances [e.g., weakness of will may rest on the lack of decisiveness, or on an exaggerated readiness to decide or delight in deciding, combined with an inadequately developed persistence, vision, or foresight], then many such "properties" are really not properties at all, but merely the outcome of circumstances, resulting from the encounter of a person with a given situation. If this is true, then our judgments of other people's facial expressions are generally subject to a profusion of presuppositions and weaknesses. Most such descriptions, based on a figure of speech, use "concepts" derived from the human sphere, which are not really concepts but reproofs or eulogies. In this way we form our standards. The value system of our upbringing, of our culture, guides us unnoticed. And although our judgment of our everyday environment proceeds by the most convenient pragmatic principles, how helpless we are when first faced with a foreign environment! Interpretation is an art; not even psychopathology and the psychology of race should forget this, if they wish to avoid being mired in Pharisaism.)

Therefore we must guard against being too eager to go from a reading of mime to physiognomic interpretation and to conceive the physiognomy as a congealed mime. But on the other hand, the closeness of the two possibilities of interpretation is illuminating for the nature of mimic expression. We have described such expression as immediate, involuntary, and not intrinsically related to the presence of others, i.e., without referential character. Accordingly, we find characteristic mimic forms of expression wherever the appropriate anatomical and psychological conditions are present. Naturally, custom, ceremonial, deportment can banish from society or suppress a given expression and intensify or stylize another. And at all times the possibility exists that man may shape his natural miming into the material of his gesticulatory language. Seen from without and for the average consciousness, the transition from *mimus* to *gestus* is gradual. But this gradual transition from natural mime to deliberate (or at any rate convention-governed) gesticulatory language cannot blur the essential difference between the two modes of expression.

If gesture expresses something because we mean something *by* it, mimic expression (like the facial) *has* a significance because an agitation (a condition or a welling-up emotion of the internal state) is externally reflected *in* it. The furrowed brow, the flashing eye, the outthrust chin, and the clenched fist are components of an immediately expressive image whose transparency refers "on its own" to an emotional state and is not first produced by the interposition of the person (as in the case of a gesture). In many cases this transparency is not plain enough to ensure the intelligibility of the expression. Also, if we do not recognize the situation to which it belongs, the expressive image as such almost always leaves several possibilities of interpretation open. But this does not affect the expressionality itself. We can be mistaken about the meaning of a facial or bodily expression, but not that it is such an expression.[9]

The immediacy and involuntary character of mimic expression is apparent in its irreplaceability and in the inseparability of the expressive movement from its content. This character of natural development in organic relation to the psychophysical organization of the person can again be explained in terms of the contrast with gesture. Bowing, waving, shaking hands, placing the hand over the heart, and so on can be replaced (by other gestures or by words). They are intended as replaceable gestures and are understood as such. Their replaceable character is synonymous with their separability from the intention in a given case. Even emphatically mimic expressive movements such as frowning, head-shaking, smiling, and expressions of liking, respect, disgust, and the like testify to this separable and replaceable character when we use them as gestures. On the other hand, as mimic expressive movements per se, they appear irreplaceable, fused with their intention (or significant content), and inseparable from the unity of the expressive whole.

Moreover, this interpenetration of mental content and bodily expressive appearance is so complete that it becomes impossible to grasp the content of an emotional state, a mood, disposition, or inclination, entirely for itself and without the possibilities of expression given once and for all by the organization of the body. We have here no means of deciding whether or not the expressive image, e.g., of an explosive force,* presents a form "suitable" to the content of anger. For we are acquainted with anger only in its appropriate outbreak, even when its complete realization is suppressed. We do not know, therefore, how deeply the physically given means of expression and expressive surfaces of the face and figure and the disposition of the limbs determine

* E.g., "bursting with rage."

the inner configuration of the psyche's agitations. Could joy develop as joy without a pressure upward and outward, rage as rage without a savage tendency to thrust forward, dread as dread without a tendency to shrink and flee downward and backward? Without the morphological external component (possible *expression*), the actual inner state does not attain that distinctness which is part of its nature as joy, anger, grief, dread, and the like.

The James-Lange theory of the emotions is certainly correct insofar as it stresses the indistinguishability of the genuinely psychic constituent and that derived from the proprioceptive sensations which we receive from those parts of the body involved in a given expression. Joy without sensations of expansion and extension in the region of the breast is not joy at all. (Whence, however, the step of equating the emotion itself with the somatic sensations does not conclusively follow.) To this extent, Klages, the strongest proponent of the "intelligibility" of the expressive image, is correct when he states that the body is the outward appearance of the mind, and the mind the meaning of the living body. In expressive mime, psychological content and physical form are related to each other as poles of a unity, which cannot be separated and reduced to the relation of sign and thing signified, of husk and grain, without destroying their organic, immediate, and spontaneous living unity.

A common token of all configurations in the area of mimic—and we may also add here, of facial—expression is that lack of differentiation between content and form which forbids our seeing them in a relation of external conjunction. There are morose and joyful, sunny and anxious, malicious and good-natured faces and features, i.e., images of psychic transparency, a plastic art and a plasticity of direct symbolism. However much experience and delicacy of judgment * need be presupposed in order to read faces and features, however easily they deceive us, and—we must not forget— no matter how great a person's ability may be to control mime and physiognomy as gestures in order to impersonate another or to conceal his true inner self behind a convincing symbolism, still the symbolic plasticity of

* *physiognostisches Taktgefühl:* One could coin the term "physiognostic," corresponding to the neologism "physiognosis" in Michael Polanyi, *Personal Knowledge: Towards a Post-Critical Philosophy* (Chicago: University of Chicago Press, 1958). However, the meaning is clear in this case if the adjective is omitted.—M. G.

an immediate and involuntary expression exists: a particular mode of irreplaceable bodily expression.

Irreplaceability, immediacy, and involuntariness give laughing and crying the character of true expressive movements. Their original link with the emotions—never mind for now with which—forces itself upon our eyes and ears with irresistible authority. With scarcely any other expression is it easier for us to distinguish the authentic from the inauthentic. The aural impression may control the optical; more than this, it holds us in its spell, it is contagious. Only by self-control can we continue to be disinterested spectators in the presence of genuine laughing or crying. More forcefully than any other expressive pattern, the laughing and crying of our fellow man grip us and make us partners of his agitation without our knowing why. Corresponding to this powerful effect, there is on the side of the laughing or crying person himself that transport, that overpowering of himself by his own expression, which is just as contrary to its detached application in the sense of gesticulatory language as it is to its arbitrary production. Yet laughter is nevertheless always easier to evoke than weeping. Even the great actors do not always succeed in producing real tears.

Thus laughing and crying seem to exhibit the essential characteristics of mimic expression in its purest form and greatest intensity. The question of their opposition, i.e., the question, therefore, of the emotions to which they give a "suitable" expression, must be resolved according to the principles which are valid for the understanding of patterns of expressive mime in general. However, we need make this attempt but once to convince ourselves that the region of "mimic expressive movements" is still too broad to delimit accurately the peculiar phenomenon of laughing and crying. With their delimitation relative to the domain of gesture and language, we shall have fulfilled only the first condition which opens the way to a real understanding.

2. The Notion of Expressive Movement in the Light of Action

Every analysis of expression must be prepared for an objection when it attempts to arrive at precise boundaries between modes of expression: that after all the difference between communicative gesture and expressive mime is obviously only subjective, since it is dependent on the intention of the individual who has something to express. But then such subjectivity of intention puts the criteria of whether it is a matter of gesticulatory language or true expressive mime at the discretion of the observer.

However, this inference is not convincing. From the subjectivity of intention of the expression, it does not follow that the judgment of the observer is arbitrary. On the contrary, he has a positive feeling for what is gesture and what is immediate expression. No matter how easy it may be for the person confronting him to change from one category of expression to the other (and in this way a misleading situation can arise at any time), still the opposition between the categories is unaffected. It is of the nature of an expression to have "two sides": the bodily configuration of the visually presented appearance and the inner intention. It is a prejudice to hold that, because of its subjectivity, the inner component is less objective than the outer. Rather, this inner component belongs just as much to the objectively necessary constituents of an expression as does its bodily appearance, which indeed can only be recorded by means of an objectifying *agency*, e.g., photography.

This may easily be established if we attempt to interpret expressive images presented in isolation. If the development is missing in which the expression before us normally flows to its full meaning, above all, if the situation in which we usually encounter the expression is absent, we have the greatest difficulty in understanding it. We see an image, but we cannot see through it. The circle of its interpretation will not close, and we grope in uncertainty. One and the same mime fits, say, "indignation" and "perception of an unpleasant odor," or "sleepiness" and "reflection." Thus the significance of the expression depends on its being developed through, and embedded in, a definite situation no less than on the significance of the expressive image itself. And this distinction contains, in fact, a genuine problem, the problem of the morphology and dynamics of expression.[10]

The objection mentioned above brings us to this question: Is there a delimitable store of forms which evoke typical expressive traits in posture and movement? Can we reduce the possibilities of expressive mime (particularly of the face, but also of the voice and the entire body) to certain basic forms? According to what principle is expressive mime in general differentiated from other movements of the body; according to what principle does it develop?

As long as there has been a serious effort to treat facial expression and mime scientifically, whatever interests were involved, whether practical, in the training of actors or the interpretation of character, or theoretical, in aesthetics and psychology—this question has dominated the theory of expression. The answers that have been discovered are limited. They proceed essentially from two standpoints: from the contrast between expression and action and from the expressive harmony between inner and outer. Sometimes the biological riddle of the function of expression comes to the fore, sometimes the psychological riddle of how what is inside manages to shape the outside.

For a conception convinced of the functionalism and economy of organic life there are only goal-directed actions, functional reactions. From this point of view, the phenomena of expression are completely paradoxical. For what does an animal, and man in particular, get out of his miming? We might think of the goal of mutual understanding, but language, or its offshoot, gesticulatory language, serves this end. It is not the case that in place of the language which animals lack they have at their disposal a correspondingly heightened, richer expressive life (even if we restrict ourselves to those most akin to man and most open to his understanding, the higher mammals). Rather man, who—since he can speak—needs it least, possesses the most differentiated power of mime. Furthermore, mime in its typical individual forms, in its appearance and subsequent disappearance, is beyond the range of will. Expression begins of itself, involuntarily, often treacherously, overpowering, confusing, and interrupting every now and then the controlled attitude, the planned action. It comes from a different depth than does deliberately planned behavior, out of the nature of biological existence in which animals also participate—their comparatively grosser mime (so far as we have access to it) being in certain basic forms similar to ours.

Thus, unless we do violence to their nature, we must not interpret expressive movements as purposive actions whose goal is mutual understanding or signaling. Hence they threaten to disappear entirely from the perspective of function and economy. In order to prevent this and to reconcile the ateleological nature of mime with the demands of a teleology of organic nature, the attempt has been made to derive expressive movement from purposive action, but to respect its peculiar import and to find a basis for its existence alongside purposive actions.

The theories of Darwin, Piderit, and Klages essentially follow this idea. According to Darwin, expression is the functionless remainder of a function which, considered phylogenetically, once had a use. According to Piderit, it is an action with a fictitious object. According to Klages, it is a likeness of an action.

Everything living must have its purpose, and if it does not have one at present, it must at least have had one: the famous theory of vestigial organs loosens the rigid subjection of the organism to the teleological principle by referring back to its phylogenetic past, but without surrendering that principle. Just as every individual in the course of its life drags along with it vestiges of its origin and traces of its development, even though in changed circumstances they have long been functionless, so also does the species, so also does man. Darwinism has taught us to recognize the traces of the past in a given organization. His principle is especially helpful in cases of obvious disturbance of functional harmony or total absence of function; see, for example, the appendix, which—so far as we know—has as its sole purpose raising the incomes of surgeons. But if there are organs in process of reversion, then there can also be functions undergoing a like process, functions which had a significance thousands of years ago, when their bearer was a different, more primitive creature and had to use these functions to carry on the struggle for existence. Now they still cling to him as frozen habits, weapons which have lost their purpose, antiquated contrivances of an unwieldy architecture, in which a new life has long since pressed into the light.

With this idea of the vestigial function, Darwin gave the theory of expression of emotion a surprising turn. An example: In the expressive image of rage, the contortion of the curve of the mouth predominates, so that the row of front teeth is not uncovered symmetrically, but the canines are characteristically laid bare on either right or left. Why this aimless grimace? Darwin gives a phylogenetic answer. Man is descended from apelike ancestors whose teeth included highly developed canines. For attack and defense these had special value, to say nothing of their value as a threat to their foe. If the animal became angry, the movement of the mouth then initiated an appropriate action. This movement survived the process of reversion of the canines and in this way came to have a purely demonstrative character, which confronts us today only as a now unintelligible mime, accompanying the corresponding subjective agitation.

In similar fashion the wrinkling of the forehead in anger or intense deliberation can be traced back to the original intense stare at an enemy, or the expression of a sweet or bitter face to the corresponding sensations of taste. More problematic, however, are laughing and crying. For crying, matters may be put right by saying that it represents a reflex-type defensive reaction of the eye against disturbing environmental effects on the cornea. The secretion of tears has the purpose of removing painful and damaging foreign bodies from the eye. In addition, they occur as reflex reactions after serious and painful actions on the eye and the region surrounding it (according to the law of the coexcitation of adjacent parts). From here on, the sensation of pain in general is associated with the secretion of tears, even when the eyes are not immediately affected, and finally this association becomes so firm that it even survives the change from physical to subjective pain.

Apart from the artificiality and unverifiability of derivations of this kind, we must note that they have to be supported by principles other than that of the acquisition by an action of vestigial character. We find here the principle of coexcitation, of the association between similar sensations and reactions (a principle employed especially in the variant of functionally associated habits), and also the principles of direct elimination of excess excitation ("nervous energy") and of contrast. More important than these, however, is the principle which Piderit, almost two decades before Darwin and independently of all phylogenetic speculation, made the central point of the theory of mime: the notion that expression is an action with a fictitious object.

Even the theory of vestiges must face the question why certain actions keep pace with the development of the individual and the species, i.e., disappear with alteration and make way for new actions, while certain other actions do not disappear but undergo a metamorphosis to expression before they vanish wholly from the memory of nature. Why do particular motor forms survive, though vestigial and indistinct, and others not? According to Darwin this is due to emotional agitation, which builds a bridge between the individual of the present and of the past. Dread and delight, rage and greed, pleasure and pain form the essential component in elemental "e-motions" which extends from prehistory right up to the differentiated affective and psychological dynamics of modern man. With them he remains bound to, and comparable with, his primitive ancestor. The elemental impulses produce the same drives now as in primitive times; and it is only our changed organization and biological situation that give a modified response to them, in which, like a shadow, the earlier response shows through.

If for Darwin, accordingly, this change in significance from earlier action to later expression appears as the consequence of these actions' becoming rudimentary, on the basis of surviving elemental emotions, Piderit proceeds, conversely, from the change in significance and from there projects the image of the current expression. He takes seriously as such the intention which is realized in the expression, and only interprets it—in view of the domination of all life by teleology—as action, more precisely, as a substitute action [*Ersatzhandlung*].

Such action is related to true action as representation is to reality, as fiction is to a real goal. In expression man only acts as if he were pursuing a goal, while in action he seriously achieves a goal.

The basis for the emergence of such substitute forms Piderit sees, not in an independent tendency, say, in the love of play or in an excess of imagination, but in the existence of representations as well as of sensations and in the fact that identical or similar feeling-tone awakens identical or similar movements. Our sense impressions lead to reactions, which again have sense impressions as their goal, the pleasant to such as are supposed to prolong them or evoke them afresh, the unpleasant to such as aim to eliminate them and prevent them in the future. To every sphere of sense impressions belong corresponding reactions—to sensations of taste, movements of the mouth; to visual impressions, movements of the eyes, etc.—with which they are linked according to the principle of functionally associated habits. If now a feeling arises whose occasion is not a sense impression but some idea or other, it still awakens the cognate reactions as if it were a case of real sensations.

There is no lack of appropriate metaphors. We accord to sweetness, sourness, or bitterness of mien the same pregnance of meaning as to sensations of taste, and show just as little reluctance to talk of bitter sorrow, a distasteful task, and sweet love. We have in general, as Wundt has pointed out, a remarkable predilection for characterizing mental states by concepts taken from the sphere of taste: we frequently describe life as "bitter" or "sweet"; we describe people as "soured" or "embittered." This predilection is not accidental, but accords with the stronger and more differentiated affective resonance of sensations of taste as compared with impressions of the other senses. In fact, optical, aural, and even olfactory impressions are never able to attain this immediate expressive effect, since the motor reactions of the cheek and mouth parts, and no doubt the region around the eyes as well, immediately respond to the stimulation of the mucous membrane of the mouth and cheeks and of the tear ducts. The affective resonance of the other sense qualities is naturally more limited, for the motor reactions of the nose and even of the eyes, to say nothing of the external ear, have far fewer possibilities. But still there is wrinkling one's nose in disgust, disdain, and scorn; there are also the blinking and intense staring characteristic of close attention and reflection, the wide-open eyes of joy, boldness, and enthusiasm, the listless, sunken eyelids of boredom, and, finally, the attentive attitude we find with deliberation, recollection, and reflection.

It proves very useful to Piderit's theory that in the individual case the difference between authentic expression and expressive gesture is difficult to determine. Here the image of the expression is intelligible from the point of view of action or stimulus-determined reaction, even if there is no unconscious transference to build a bridge from what is sensibly present to its representation, but the gesture arises in full consciousness of its metaphorical character. On the other hand, Piderit imposed a limitation on his theory. He wanted to recognize only purposeful reactions or actions, and would allow, moreover, only sense impressions to serve as their causes and ends. In order to understand on this basis the origin and "meaning" of expressive mime, he had to construct an unconscious and involuntary mechanism of transference, and he burdened his theory with this assumption.

From the standpoint of psychology, neither the monopoly of goal-directed reactions, and therefore of actions, nor the exclusive power of sense impressions to induce reactions appears tenable. Klages succeeded in freeing the nugget of truth in Piderit's theory from its delusive covering. He was able to do this because, in opposition to pragmatism and sensationalism, he ventured, for one thing, to recognize the independence of a symbolic intent in expressions and (contrary to his predecessors) to interpret the theory of expressive movement from this standpoint.

Above all, according to Klages, what is decisive is not the sense impression but its pleasantness or offensiveness, i.e., its feeling-tone. Compared with this tone, the inducing sensation has only representative value. Language (or facial expression) has this value in mind when it suggests, for example, that we cannot see or smell someone.* A bitter lesson, a distasteful task, an illuminating idea, or a sweet melody has these qualities, not in virtue of a mechanism of association and transfer but as genuine affective values. That is, in the sensation, let us say, of tasting bitter grapefruit and in the experience of a bitter lesson primordially related factors are involved (intermodal properties,[11] as they have been called), and it is to these that a bitter grimace gives expression.

If sweetness, bitterness, sourness, and the like are naturally evident tones of our experience, tones of an affective character which do not leave us indifferent but put us in a mood, attract or repel us, then the derivation of the corresponding expressive movement from reactions to sense impressions becomes superfluous. Long before the above-mentioned investigations of the modern psychology of sensation, Klages had recognized in this affective resonance of sensory life an important support for his theory of expression. Mime can maintain its similarity to a given action without on that account originating from an action or (fictively) imitating it. Although it "resembles" an action, still it does not share its goal-related, goal-oriented intention, to which Piderit, with his theory of the imaginary object of the expression, wanted to hold fast.

With this, the possibility is also given of recognizing an independent psychological tendency in addition to that which leads to action and appears under the law of end and goal, a tendency that is realized in expression and has its own "law of significance." In this law lies the key to the understanding of expression. Klages finds it in the types of drive [*Antriebsformen*] characteristic of the feelings, which are said to determine the development of a particular bearing and physiognomy.

As long as the psychology of feeling fitted its task of investigation into the framework of a "consciousness" populated with sensations, representations, and associations, it sought either to reduce feelings to the play of these elements or to banish them to the sphere of the unconscious. Feelings were something in-

* The nearest to this in English is: "I can't stand the sight of him."—M. G.

tangible, had no precise outlines, and above all they were passive states without any dynamic components. Klages broke with this prejudice, characteristic of a positivistic, intellectualistic psychology. Because he recognized in every feeling a characteristic stimulus-form, Klages restored to its original intensity that immense region of feeling and emotional life which sustains, oppresses, permeates, and so often drowns out our consciousness by recognizing in every feeling a characteristic drive. This is discharged in the elementary expression, on which it thereby sets its seal. Body (as the organ of expression) is soul, just as soul (as drive) is the sense of the living body. Joy is what uplifts us, enlarges, presses outward, opens; rage is what clenches us, closes, urges us to strike out (an urge that is realized in blows or in screaming).

Our objection that the form of drive can be grasped only through its discharge and cannot be depicted in itself Klages can even turn into a support for his theory of the unity of soul and body. As long as the theory takes into account the limits set by the objection and does not affirm a (preestablished) harmony between the emotional state and its expression—between magnitudes which we cannot isolate relative to each other—it restricts itself to the report of a condition. The feeling and its expressive image are experienced in their adequation. Thus the problem of the dynamics and morphology of those images is shifted to the level of feelings and the drives appropriate to them.

The only thing that continues to be remarkable—also in Klages' interpretation—is the relation between expression and action. To be sure, expression is no longer presented as a derivative or offshoot of action but takes its place, as equally justified because equally primary, alongside it. But the expression still resembles the action; it acts as the symbol of an action, or in place of it. It is related to action, though at the distance of a likeness. The same drive can be discharged in action or in expressive movement, depending on the circumstances, the degree of inhibition, the weighing of the consequences. In expressive movement the tension does indeed produce an actual discharge, but, in contrast to its real execution by means of action, it leads in reality to nothing, but, in symbolic abridgment, brings forth a substitute. The tension is directly intercepted, as if in a kind of short circuit, and thus appears as expressive movement: an image, a materialization, and to that extent a symbol of the inner drive, a symbol that—by the *tertium comparationis* of precisely this form of drive—presents itself as the likeness of an action.

3. The Expressive Character of Laughing and Crying

It is no accident that in interpretations of expressive movement which in any sense take action as their perspective laughing and crying play a very minor part. To what fictive object can they be coordinated except by far-fetched analogies? What real action could they "portray" in symbolic abridgment?

Even the picture which they directly present exhibits only a sector of the whole expressive complex as it emerges in the total development of laughing and crying. In contrast to emotion-guided expressions, in which a mood, an affective state, an agitation runs its course, radiating, as it were, into a range of expressive movements, laughing and crying lack this transition from inner to outer. We are capable of laughing or crying—and here they reveal their partnership because they are parts of a particular genus of human expression—only if we give way to them. *We burst out laughing* and *allow ourselves to burst into tears*. While the lack of transition in laughter is readily apparent in expressions like "bursting out," "splitting," "exploding," and the like, in crying it is concealed by the peculiarly reflexive behavior of the weeping person, who must let himself dissolve in tears in order to find his solution. The occasion for laughter overtakes and overpowers us. Often we must hold ourselves in by force to keep from bursting out laughing. The occasion for crying can also overtake us suddenly and make demands on our self-control. Only we are not delivered up to it with the same directness. The occasion moves us, and only when we have given way to that affecting movement do the tears come.

This lapsing and falling into tears and laughter reveals, especially with a view to the peculiarly autonomous process which then begins, and which frequently resists suppression and direction even to the point of complete exhaustion, a loss of control, a breakdown of the equilibrium between man and his physical existence. A sudden and powerful outburst of feeling can drive us to unthinking expressive movements; we are then no longer masters of ourselves and no longer have our wits about us. But the animation of the body reaches its high point in this situation. Even if the unity of the person, the control of his intellectual and moral center, is endangered, the expressive transparency of the body in such circumstances is at any rate not to be surpassed: a "minus" for man as a person, a "plus" for him as an ensouled-embodied creature.

Exactly the opposite is true in laughing and crying. The living transparency of the body reaches its lowest point in them. Bodily reactions emancipate themselves; man is shaken by them, buffeted, made breathless. He has lost the relation to his physical existence; it withdraws from him and does with him more or less what it will. At the same time we feel this loss as the expression of, and the answer to, a particular kind of situation. Our internal equilibrium is also at an end, but this time the "minus" is debited to the soul-body unit and not to the person.

In contrast to mimic expressive movement, the genus of laughing and crying presents itself as a kind of manifestation in which *the loss of control in the whole context* has expressive value. The disorganization of the relation between man and his physical existence is not willed, to be sure, but—although it sets in in an overwhelming way—it is still not merely accepted and endured. On the contrary, it is understood as expressive movement and significant reaction. Even in the catastrophe which overtakes his relation to his own body, a relation which he otherwise controls, man triumphs and confirms himself as man. By slipping as if by accident into a physical process and giving way to it, a process opaque in itself which runs its course compulsively, by the disorganization of his inner balance, man at once forfeits the relation to his body *and* reestablishes it. The effective impossibility of finding a suitable expression and an appropriate answer *is* at the same time the only suitable expression, the only appropriate answer.

From this we can better understand the claim to see expressive movement and action in one and the same perspective without blurring their natural boundaries. They correspond to the normal case of problematic situations which permit an answer, in terms of our use of our bodies (consciously or unconsciously, voluntarily or involuntarily) as instruments. Sometimes the body serves as a sounding board and emission surface for emotions pressing for relief, sometimes as an organ of speech, sometimes as a means of signaling and an organ of gesture, sometimes as a means of locomotion, of grasping, propping, carrying, pushing, and so on. Everywhere the nature of the situation permits man, indeed compels him, to find an unequivocal relation to the ambiguity of his physical existence as body in the body *in the light of this very ambiguity.* If, however, the situation cannot be brought to fulfillment, if it becomes unanswerable in itself, then speech and gesture, action and expressive movement, break down. Then there is nothing more to be done with the situation; we have no more to say to it, we don't know where we are with it. In such defective circumstances that point of reference must also vanish which man needs if he is to find a relation to his physical existence.

Disorientation is the natural consequence. But it is not a matter here of simply orienting oneself within the compass of an otherwise straightforward situation, as in the case, say, of someone who has lost his way or the thread of a conversation, or who no longer finds himself at home in a text or in a social gathering. It is rather a matter of situations in the face of which no meaningful answer, however constituted—whether through expressive movement, gesture, language, or action—is possible. With the disappearance of the fulcrum that would permit an equilibrium in the ambiguity of man's physical existence, disorganization is then necessarily present.

But this disorganization looks different according to whether or not the unmanageability of the situation has a life-threatening character. Situations which are both *unanswerable* and *threatening* arouse *vertigo.* Man capitulates as a person, he loses his head. Symptoms which are known to arise from giddiness, such as perspiring, nausea, and fainting, can, as we know, arise in similar crises of a higher order. The expression "my head is swimming" is entirely adequate to describe such situations.

Unanswerable and *nonthreatening* situations, on the other hand, arouse *laughing* or *crying.* Man capitulates as a soul-body unit, i.e., as a living creature; he loses the relation to his physical existence, but he does not capitulate as a person. He does not lose his head. To the unanswerable situation he still finds—by virtue of his eccentric position, because of which he is not wholly merged in any situation—the only answer still possible: to draw back from the situation and free himself from it. The body, displaced from its relation to him, takes over the answer, no longer as an instrument of action, language, gesture, or expressive movement, but as body. In losing control over his body, in giving up a relation to it, man still attests to his sovereign understanding of what cannot be understood, to his power in weakness, to his freedom and greatness under constraint. Even here he still knows how to find an answer, even where there is nothing more to answer. He has, if not the last word, still the last card to play, whose loss is his gain.

Laughing and crying are neither gestures nor expressive movements, and yet they have expressive character. Their opacity, and in a measure their meaninglessness, i.e., their lack of sharp definition and articulation, is precisely what is essential to their expressive meaning. In contrast to blushing or turning pale, which are more closely related to them than to expressive movement, they express an answer which is manifest in the way it becomes audible. If, on the one hand, this attests the eruptive onset, the penetrating depth of disorganization, and the lack of inhibition of their physical occurrence, so, on the other hand, it indicates something which should not be overlooked, namely, their social component—a component which has been interpreted, not indeed wholly incorrectly, but still certainly too narrowly, as having the function of a signal. We must not forget that sound includes the power of self-verification: one hears oneself. Here, indeed, the essential differences between laughing and crying begin to become evident. In crying, the tears fulfill the function of self-verification, but sobbing, whimpering, and sighing do not carry the expression by themselves.

If we wish to understand the difference between these two forms of expression, a more detailed examination of the structure of their occasions is unavoidable. Apart from the fact that we cannot understand, from what has been said so far, why there are just two forms within this strange genus of expressions, our thesis concerning their expressive character will remain at loose ends until we have been able to corroborate it in different cases. It is possible to laugh and cry for many reasons which at first sight appear to be incapable of comparison. For what do comic appearance and embarrassment, for instance, or wit and despair have in common? And yet they make us laugh. What connects pain and joy, remorse and devotion? And yet they make us cry. Besides, how will we explain that in certain situations, e.g., despair, a person can do both, or that he can err in his expression?

The progress of our analysis now depends on the insight into situations to which laughing and crying, each in its own way, provide an answer, situations of which a man both takes and gives notice, all in one: confirms and quits. There has been no lack of contrasts between the two modes of expression: We laugh only at others, we weep only about ourselves (Joh. E. Erdmann); laughter is heartless and cold, intellectual, while weeping is warm with emotion and bound to feeling (Bergson), an expression of sympathy with oneself (Schopenhauer). Nor is there any lack of analyses of occasions that arouse laughter in particular, such as the comic or the joke. But only rarely and incidentally has anyone made an effort to build a bridge between the structure of the occasion and the corresponding expressive reaction or, with this in view, to investigate even widely divergent occasions, and above all to take laughing and crying equally into account. What matters most in this connection is not so much complete enumeration as paradigmatic penetration.

3 / Occasions of Laughter

1. Expressive Movements of Joy and Titillation

Our thesis that the physical mode of expression of laughter suits the occasion and responds to it without being definitely shaped by it—and so differs essentially and not merely in degree from expressive movement—is at first sight made questionable by two possibilities of release: *joy* [*Freude*] and *titillation* [*Kitzel*]. For in both instances laughter appears as a genuine expressive movement which is stamped by an internal state in two different ways. Since joy, as a very comprehensive state of being moved and elated, can in turn have the most diverse occasions, our inquiry must consider whether the expressive movement characteristic of the joyful mood is genuine laughter and to what it is related. For it is by no means certain that the object of our joy is also the reason for our laughter.

In contrast, titillation is a narrowly circumscribed, sensuously definable state, which can be described as a type of stimulus confined to surface areas. As a releasing agent of laughter, titillation has a special interest insofar as it seems to open up possibilities of an exact analysis, oriented to the model of stimulus and response. However, if a reflex were actually at work here, then one would have to ask oneself whether laughter induced in this way could still qualify as expressive movement, let alone as true laughter.

According to the general opinion, laughter belongs to joy, gaiety, merriment, joviality, and cheerfulness. Joyful laughter as index of a relaxed and high-spirited good fellowship constantly provides this opinion with fresh support. The question of the James-Lange theory of the emotions—do we laugh because we are cheerful or are we cheerful because we laugh?—seems to be a confirmation of the expressive link between these moods and laughter. For the question of their separability makes sense only where the intimate union of the internal and its external expression makes the independence of the internal or of an allegedly internal state (the emotion of joy, etc.) seem suspect. If the expressive forms are lacking—and, as we know, this holds in general for the whole scale of affects and emotions, so far as they manifest themselves in movements involving the whole body, the face, or the voice—the corresponding emotions are also lacking (at any rate in their full development). In good part, their suppression is equivalent to their disappearance.

When our hearts leap up because we have received good news, when we are agreeably surprised because of an unexpected present or are jovial and in good spirits because for once we can break out of the gray monotony of the weight of daily care—we may laugh. But our laughter is in reality elation [*Jubeln*]. It is that unrestrained "swinging-out" of sound which follows the general, expansive thrust of the emotion of joyous excitement. The more unexpected, the more surprising the coming of the joyful event, the more liberating its effect. If we have awaited such an event long, anxiously, and in secret, then the expression of joy at its coming can also be quite different. If we still have the strength to rejoice, it will overwhelm us and move us to tears.

Elation embodies the expressive behavior of being beside oneself with happiness. As we leap up, dance about, do foolish things, make senseless gestures, are transported by rapture in all its vehemence, we break out in jubilation. Yet it is not always easy to say to what extent elation is still immediate expressive movement or already gesture. Among children and primitive peoples, the repression effected by social consideration can fall away; but where life unrolls under the eye of social convention, immediate expression is strongly braked, and gesture takes its place. But as vocal expression, elation has no specific stamp. As the unfettered discharge of overflowing emotion ("not knowing where to turn for joy," "not being able to rest for joy," etc.), it manifests itself vocally partly in sequences of sound to some extent resembling laughter. But the discriminating ear can still hear the difference. Exultation does not "peel off" a person like a volley of laughter. It has none of that automatism, both pushed and pushing, which shakes the laugher and makes him lose his breath. Thus exultation is displayed all the way from the formlessness of the unrestrained outbreak of sounds and shouts to singing "from an overflowing heart," "from the swelling breast," and ebbs away as the emotion becomes calmer.

Elation and laughter differ, but still in a fashion which permits their union: an extraordinarily good joke, an unusually comical situation, not only makes us laugh; it inspires us, it is a gift of fortune. And just as there is the exultant laugh, so there is also happy, lusty, cheerful laughter in all grades of emotional temperature, in all possible combinations of specific occasions. Moreover, we should not overlook the fact that the relaxation of a cheerful, happy, joyous mood disposes us to jest, to wit; it disposes us, in a word, not to take things seriously. Everywhere, where burdens are lifted, perspectives broadened, and limitations fallen away, man acquires the facility of putting himself at a distance from his own kind and from things. In such a disengagement the true sources of laughter—jest, humor, and wit—are revealed. All the forms of facility which we distinguish have, therefore, the significance of a climate in which man is disposed to jest and wit and is in good spirits, but laughter they do not in themselves arouse.

It is also true that in a cheerful mood laughter lacks any bitter corollary. Not taking things seriously, for the most part, remains within the bounds of inoffensiveness. We laugh easily, but the laughter is shallow. Even the most trivial occasion suffices for us to find something funny and amusing. The more unpretentious a social gathering, the greater will be its openness to such a mood. With a little alcohol it is easy to produce. People tease and make fun of one another and generally make merry. But for fun and wit to attain real depth, humor must be put to the test. Only then does laughter attain true stature because it is mixed with elation, the elation we experience when we have overcome chagrin. The lightness achieved, and at the same time tempered, by insight into the real unmanageability in the essence of things is the best climate for a laughter that surges up from within. In such rare cases (which are naturally oriented to the level of the individual and cannot be binding on all by some universal criterion) laughter becomes the movement expressive of elation. Hence arises the false impression that laughter in general is an expressive movement. In reality we are only capturing our own laughter and letting our jubilant unruliness, in search of some expression, ring out in it. In itself, elation does not lead to laughter. To think so is, again, to jump to conclusions.

The other phenomenon to which the thesis of the gesticulatory character of laughter can appeal is titillation: a narrowly circumscribed, sensuously definable state describable as a type of stimulus which—seen from the human point of view—remains superficial. One is immediately ticklish, for example, under the arms, on the soles of the feet, at the nape of the neck—in places, therefore, which are not in general exposed to light, ephemeral tactile stimuli and which occupy clearly demarcated areas of the body schema. But one also experiences tickling when a fly crawls over his skin; carbonic acid tickles the nose, and delicate dishes tickle the palate. In a derived sense, we speak of ticklish situations or affairs, of erotic titillation, of a titillation of the nerves in sensation. In all these forms some common genus must be exerting its characteristic power, which on occasion forces us to laugh.

Tickling is an ambivalent stimulus, at the same time pleasant and unpleasant in its overtones. In it, alluring and irritating factors counterbalance each other. It is this continual fluctuation of attraction and repulsion, this inequilibrium of pleasure and its opposite, presenting a continuous fluctuation and oscillation, that constitutes the essence of titillation, whether I feel it in the soles of my feet or in watching an automobile race. It is not the intensity of the stimuli or impressions which determines the quality of the titillation but the ambivalence, which, to be sure, can arise in very different ways and—as the use of the word in its metaphorical sense explains—is not bound to the zone of physical sensations. Those who venture into danger, for example, because they want to "taste the thrill" are seeking the ambivalence of titillation. Those who love the suggestive, the dissolute, the lascivious have been captivated by the attraction of the ticklish. The erotic sphere has this attraction in a double sense: as a region of ambivalent stimulation in sensuous experience as well as in the mental contact of play, of flirtation, and also, as an "open secret," as a hidden omnipresence in social relations which can only be playfully "alluded to" under the authority of repressive norms.

In the sphere of touch, weak stimuli in a narrowly circumscribed space give the impression of a tickling sensation. The lack of clarity and the surface character awaken at one and the same time a striving for greater precision and for removal of the "stimulus." To some extent, the mucous membranes of the nose and mouth react in still another way. Certain tastes and odors tickle the palate through their piquant qualities. Gently repellent and attractive factors mutually supplant one another and awaken the appetite for plain and robust fare. The titillating quality of sensations of sensual pleasure finds their immediate expression in the motor aspects of the sexual act. In the antagonism of painful and pleasurable elements the seeds of possible perversions are sown. The question of whether it is meaningful to speak of titillation in the spheres of sight and hearing may be left undecided. The concept is employed occasionally to characterize a certain cheerful dissonance found in musical impressionism. However, with regard to the function of sight, which is dependent on distance and precision, the possibility of ambivalent fulfillment seems foreign, even in cases where we are faced with the phenomena of glittering and shimmering.

An individual concerned with titillation is in search of "stimulation," and even in affective and intellectual matters, he is still a sensuous person. The man of pleasure is bound exclusively to no particular sphere, for to him sport and war, politics and erotics, books and pictures are all basically the same as a good dish. Only two things make this type (whose villainy is basically out of fashion) endurable: aesthetic culture or initiative. Cultivation of taste attenuates the danger of an overemphasis on sensuality. Initiative frees it of the repugnant trait of passive irresponsibility. It provides a kind of ethical compensation for the lack of a serious moral sense. But the man who prizes above all else the titillation of great danger finally pays his price for it. In both tendencies, sensuality has been, if not overcome, at best molded into an attitude that no longer adheres to the "lower" regions of sensation linked to specific organs. The unrestrained freedom of sensuous expression disappears.

But in moments of sensuous irritability which undergo their characteristic climax in titillation, that feeling breaks out as tittering laughter. The mime that belongs to it, with the eyelids almost closed and the mouth stretched wide, finds its vocal complement in that sequence of sound-pulses which bears a confusing resemblance to laughter. If one is especially ticklish, then this tittering is evoked easily, like a reflex. Such tittering, which also appears on other occasions as stifled laughter, is associated with the attitude of sneaking off, of making oneself small, a symbolic movement of retreat executed by the skin, i.e., the sensory surface.

Tittering or giggling is undoubtedly a genuine expressive movement. Within the sphere of mime, the voice responds involuntarily to the titillating quality of the stimulus. From this quality it takes the stamp of oscillation and superficiality. But it is still not laughter. The fact that laughter, if suppressed, can become tittering does not mean that tittering as the expression of "tickling" is a primitive form of laughter. The difference of significance in both cases is not to be ignored.

Nevertheless, the expressive movement of tittering discloses a significant tendency in laughter itself as a mode of expression. In laughter something of the character of expressive movement is assimilated and elaborated. The eruptive character and jerkiness of laughter point to a certain kinship between its occasions and the occasion of tittering, namely, the ambivalence of titillation.[12] However, while here the ambivalence has the quality of a stimulus and remains sensuously bound (be it noted, even in the transference to other orders of reality, e.g., sensations of danger, suggestive situations, etc.), there, that is, wherever the response of laughter is appropriate, ambivalence develops into ambiguity, the equivocality of the comic and of the joke, into the situation of embarrassment and despair which can no longer be controlled.

In connection with this, there is yet another important source of confusion to be noted. Real laughter can grow out of tittering if a person finds his own ticklishness—comic. In tickling, we find ourselves delivered over to an ambivalent stimulus-state which stands in a proper relation neither to the releasing cause, e.g., a tactile stimulus, nor to ourselves. We find ourselves in a perplexity we cannot master. The incongruity of the resultant situation, in which we are caught by an insignificant stimulus, at once pleasant and annoying, has a comic effect. We discover ourselves as prisoners of the body, as in cases where we stumble, behave clumsily, conduct ourselves awkwardly. Then what was originally expressive tittering turns suddenly into real laughter and so makes it look as if the tittering itself had begun as laughter. But in reality the situation has acquired a comic appearance, and the expressive movement of tittering has been supplanted by true laughter.

2. Play

Play has a specific relationship to laughter. But in this connection we should not think first of all of highly developed board and card games, which are bound to complicated rules, nor of outdoor games which have the characteristics of sport. Here skill and attentiveness are demanded to such a degree that neither energy nor distance remains over to be utilized by surplus expressions. The space between the player and his game is here supplanted by concentration on tactical and strategic problems. The sphere of play is deprived of its freely creative phantasy, along with its determination not to take things seriously, and appears instead as a fixed field of work, as an arena and a playground [*Spielraum*] with so and so many possibilities and prohibitions. In the forefront here we find performance, style, scoring, and speed.

It is quite otherwise with the simple play resulting from elementary relations to the environment and to our contemporaries, a type of play which children, above all, slip back into again and again and which occurs in part even among the higher animals in such primitive tendencies as mock combat, wrestling, or preoccupation with rolling, stretching, seesawing, or otherwise capricious things. Man takes full advantage of this controllable capriciousness with swings, seesaws, whirling, playing ball, gymnastic games, and so on. Without further ado, it is clear that the simple release of this romping is a source of pleasure and of jubilation. And just as apparent, of course, is the comic appearance of awkwardness detected in oneself or in others. This point will be separately dealt with later on. But: how does it happen that play as such induces laughter?

The answer follows from that ambivalence which we have already met in the phenomenon of titillation, admittedly in a very exaggerated form, but one which obviously opens up far-reaching perspectives. Ambivalence or double meanings need not appear only as the quality of a stimulus that is at once pleasing and displeasing, gratifying and irksome. It can determine the character of a *situation* which we see as in suspension because it depends on our creative readiness and power and at the same time links these in capricious autonomy. We are at once both free and not free, we bind and are bound. Between us and the object (the thing or the friend) an ambivalent relation prevails, of which we are both master and yet not master because we are just as much its prisoner as it is under our control. Such a relation is established by and against our wills in play.

Play is always playing with something that also plays with the player,[13] a paradoxical relation which entices us to commit ourselves, yet without becoming so firmly established that individual choice is completely lost. Nevertheless, the risk of such a change exists at every moment. The enticing, image-like [*bildhafte*] bond then vanishes, and the unambiguous moves in to take its place: play becomes action in earnest: chasing, catching, and wrestling turn into fighting, the image is displaced by reality. As long as we only act as if . . . , as long as we appeal to qualities of things that we can easily picture—their rocking and swinging, their rolling and dancing, the narrowness of the tightrope, the smoothness of the ground, the slipperiness of the slide, the elasticity of the ball—the bond is present. But if we overlook its resonance, these are all transformed into their serious quality, into useful objects with unambiguous reality.

These qualities—their image-like character and the fact that we can appeal to them—are the essential properties of play objects or playmates. A stretched rubber band which I hold in tension so that it resists me reveals these properties immediately. I concentrate on nothing else about this thing except its elasticity and, furthermore, not on this (as a technician might, for example) as on a property; rather, I go along with it. Just as it appeals to me, so I reply to it. It draws me under its spell insofar as I give myself up to it.

This bond, which confines itself entirely to the vital level of pure reciprocity and the immediate values of impressions, and is weakened neither by the pale cast of thought, i.e., by objectivity, nor by the aspect of intention and purpose, is in keeping with the drives of many animals, especially hunters, and here especially with the youthful phase with its still undirected impulse toward movement and its still abundant surplus energy (to all of which Buytendijk in particular has drawn attention). Naturally, within the framework of their actual environment, animals, in comparison with man, have only limited possibilities of play at their disposal. Occasionally they also play with their own bodies, as with a dog chasing its tail. At the same time, they pass far more easily than man, and without a real break, from seriousness to play and from play to seriousness (seriousness of which they never become conscious as such, since they only have to do with things in use, like food, like prey, enemies, dangers, enticements, obstacles, partners, prospects in their field of movement, hiding places, and so on: in short, with *circumstances* and not with objects as such).

To man, on the other hand, the sphere of play stands in contrast to the sphere of seriousness. He lives in the consciousness of authenticity. Even as a child, he can distinguish, in virtue of his eccentric position toward the world, the genuinely objective, the real, the possible, and the necessary from the image-like appeal of vital claims. He lacks in childhood only the intellectual development to enable him to survey things within the sphere of the serious in their real context and to judge the significance of his actions. But this deficiency in insight and knowledge makes itself felt only as uncertainty in the *delimitation* of the province of the nonserious, of play and imagination, or as vagueness of *articulation* within the province of the serious. The distinction between these areas as such becomes clear to him in his earliest childhood, so that even in the first year of life he is capable of achievements which a chimpanzee never learns.

Over against the province of the serious (and to that extent, against it as a latent background), image-like character and the responsiveness of the play-object and the playmate appear to man as inauthentic in contrast with the authentic—and that in two ways: first as a *domain,* and then as a *bond* founded on reciprocity and paradox. The domain of play, which he enters, and then at some times leaves, is self-contained and is not continuous with reality as such: it does not lie on the same level. When we play at being Indians, then we act as if we were Indians; and if the other does not enter in, or acts out of character—takes offense at something, for instance—then he spoils the game. However, acting as if . . . is only one of the possible forms of play. In simply running after someone, this form need not be present. In swinging or balancing, it is certainly not there. Thus role-playing and camouflage can be absent without disturbing the enactment of the domain of play. But enacted it must be, since at any moment seriousness threatens to break in from the side of the authentic. The enactment of play demands—and here the other factor comes in—the readiness to be responsive and to be bound in an imaginary way, or, in other words: the will to immanence, to bind and to let oneself be bound.

To play, for man, therefore, is to hold himself in-between in two respects. For one thing he manages to play if he shuts out the reality that is invariably present: to this extent it constantly shines in on him in the closed domain of play. For another, he keeps himself in this domain only through maintenance of the unstable, intermediate state of a bond which must constantly be renewed, a bond which is both reciprocal and paradoxical, because it consists of binding and letting oneself be bound. To this ambivalence of a double in-between—between reality and appearance, binding and being bound—man reacts—with laughter.

By this statement we are of course not claiming that the only reason for the cheering effect of play is to be found in the circumstances just described. Playing is also enjoyable because it eases us, relieves us of everyday pressures, and gives a free hand to our dammed-up motility and to the drive (especially strong in the young) to exercise our imaginations. Play creates opportunities for titillating situations, for nerve-tickling, and finally it is a source for the most diverse varieties of comedy. In each of these respects it can excite us to laughter. But it can also do this simply as play, merely through the attraction which the domain of illusion and of ambiguous constraint exerts on us. Actually, this motivation may never be entirely separable from the others, whether in the child or the adult. But the special pleasure in the state of suspense which prevails in play, in the instability of an equilibrium that is really no equilibrium, in the submergence in a world which derives from us and yet does not do so, which is capricious and yet subject to direction by our will—this pleasure is not to be overlooked. It is unambiguously pleasure, but pleasure in something ambiguous that does not fit in with the simple either-or of reality.

We laugh about such things, not because they appear comic or laughable to us, or because they tickle us, but because we cannot really dispose of them. The stimulating quality of the state of suspense in play results from the constant oscillation between attraction and repulsion which prevails in the relation of the player and the playmate (or play-object). Thus laughter has here something of the nature of a genuine expressive movement which reflects titillation. At the same time, however, it presents itself as a response to a situation that is no longer unequivocal, from which we step back without really wishing to free ourselves from it. Tension and irritation are immediately transformed into vocal expression, which from the point of view of the player, however, has the significance of a reaction, i.e., a reaction to a boundary situation, in contrast to the unequivocal relations with which he must usually reckon in life.

3. The Comic

The comic is related to laughter in the true sense of the term. In the occasions discussed so far, laughter appears as a reaction not yet developed in its full nature and is more or less restricted to the level of expressive gesticulation. As such, it remains partly the expression of joy, partly of sensuous excitement and titillation, and first becomes true laughter in play, through the pleasure arising from the suspension between caprice and constraint. If this account is correct, then the comic finds in laughter its appropriate response. It meets us in the richly varied forms of comic phenomena, of comical appearance and behavior, funny things and motions, of the comedy inherent in situation, word, and character, in daily life and in art, and, depending on our susceptibility to it, exerts its compulsion on us.

The determination of the comic is an ancient concern of philosophy, aesthetics, the theory of comedy, and, since the eighteenth century, of psychology also. As is inevitable with a problem of this kind, the most diverse motives and considerations have influenced the answers: moral reflections, pedagogical standpoints, and, above all, scientific and scholarly principles and prejudices. Without constant contact with the history of philosophy, psychology, education, and artistic ideals, a history of theories of comedy would remain a patchwork. Granted, the interest of its net yield would scarcely repay the trouble. For we really cannot speak of progress in the theory of the phenomenon. For every aspect, a corresponding formula comes forward, which renders, or at least catches, the essence of the comic in more or less suitable expressions. But if the aspect changes, then the expressions also fade, and from their frozen forms all life has fled. Who would deny that the aesthetics of empathy or associationist psychology, that Hegelian dialectic or the Kantian critical philosophy had not long since found an appropriate formulation for the comic? But since their horizon, their technical vocabulary, their philosophical attitude in general are for us no longer uncontested, we are not able simply to satisfy ourselves with their solutions, neither as definitive nor as preliminary. Acquaintance with past efforts does not absolve us from our own attempt to make the essence of the comic come alive in examples, especially since we are trying to understand it with reference to the reaction of laughter and only peripherally as an aesthetic category.

Admittedly, Bergson's celebrated analysis, *Le rire*, approached the phenomenon with the same intent; the only objection to it is that it investigates laughter exclusively within the horizon of the comic, a restriction which, however, detracts nothing from the insights it does provide.

According to Bergson, the range of the comic is confined to the domain of the human. Cloud and rock formations, forms of plants and animals, look funny to us (i.e., not strange and unfamiliar, but amusing and laughable) only if they somehow remind us of the human—of a face, figure, or any part of the human body. In such cases they display to us in a likeness certain traits of our total impression of man, but in a detached and autonomous way that conflicts with the animation normally required of him, i.e., inseparably associated with him as human. Thus, we do not really laugh at these characteristics as such but at the obstinacy of the human body which eludes the law of life (though only in the likeness of a natural phenomenon that evokes a memory).

Such apparently extrahuman comedy is thus basically the same as what we encounter in any of the forms of absent-mindedness or stereotypes of human behavior and nail down in caricature or imitation. Only here nature has taken over the role of the caricaturist or imitator. Thus the proposition holds that: "Attitudes, gestures, and movements of the human body are comic to the extent that in them the body reminds us of a mere mechanism." Whenever a person appears like a thing—a marionette, a doll, or a clown—when our attention is turned to his physical nature in situations in which his rational nature is in the foreground—sneezing in the middle of a speech, for instance —the comic state is present.

Why? According to Bergson, our social instinct is defending itself here. Just as, according to him, laughter is always the laughter of a group—even when I laugh for myself alone—so the comic presents an offense against the basic principle of social life: be resilient, adjust to all circumstances, control yourself. It rests on a slipping of life into mechanical stiffness; it is basically identical with the phenomenon of absent-mindedness. And laughter is the punishment for this. We deride the absent-minded person; we laugh as a rebuke, as a corrective, but also as a warning. In laughter, the presence of society in us, the social instinct, calls attention to a danger to which man is exposed through his physical existence; and while laughter punishes the offender, at the same time it heals the wound which it inflicts on him: it brings him back to life.

Inattentiveness, absent-mindedness, and inflexibility readily manifest themselves in clumsiness and rigidity of behavior and thus direct the attention of our fellow men to things which in themselves should be unobtrusive. Instead of remaining in the role of partner to which society assigns him, an "absent-minded" individual falls out of this role and becomes a spectacle to others. The reasons for this can be quite different, as can its expressions. The absent-minded professor who lives in his problems and does all sorts of silly things, who stumbles, mistakes one thing for another, and adopts stock phrases, or the victim of a wild party who fails to notice that everything around him is suddenly topsy-turvy, appears just as funny as excessive corpulence, too big a nose, or a gross eccentricity in behavior. The body naturally plays the lead as bearer of comic properties, even though *its* bearer for the most part cannot help it. They thrust themselves and him into the limelight in a way which is at odds with the human. For society does not care to be reminded of noses, ears, and feet, even though such structures are somehow necessary to life.

To the extent that sympathy or disgust does not prevail, as, for example, at the sight of the crippled or the sick, every emancipation of what is usually instrumental, whether physical or not, has a comic effect. Exaggerated ceremonial, mechanical bureaucracy, *hybris,* which substitutes human regulation for nature's, are laughable. What is decisive here is not ugliness, which repels us, or irrationality, which irritates us, but stiffness and the want of life. Every form that suppresses content, every letter that tries to trick the spirit, every function of life that oppresses life, or seems to, becomes comic. For in them all there is a conjunction that presents us with the illusion or certainty of life, together with the feeling of a mechanical arrangement.

Bergson rightly recognized that the art of the comic has always made use of the average and prefers to choose as a theme the general and the replaceable, i.e., in some sense the schematic, while serious, tragic art puts the individual at the center.

Comedies are: *L'Avare, Le Malade imaginaire, Der Schwierige;* tragedies: *Othello, Hamlet, Faust.* True, there is here no universal rule, but still a significant preference, since (to express the matter in Bergson's language) vitality is revealed in constant alteration of aspect, irreversibility in order of appearance, perfect individuality of a series closed on itself. If this vitality holds its ground against the generalizing, automaticizing power of a passion or a vice, and if behind such power the worth of the individual appears, even in his destruction, then he produces on us the effect of tragedy. On the other hand, if individuality does not assert itself against the rigidity and depersonalization of passion, if it makes no inner struggle against fate, if it falls victim to passion (and without too serious consequences), then the comic effect prevails.

What contradicts life and its uniqueness and yet can master life? Repeatability, reversibility, and ambiguity. On their employment rests the comedy of situations, words, and characters; the more natural its sources, the more irresistible its effect. Hackneyed idioms, periodic reiteration of certain phrases, and unwanted recurrences of situations are examples of repetition. Repartee, word-twisting, and even reversals of whole scenes (as in the popular case of the deceiver deceived) are examples of inversion. And mistaken identities, which the writer of farces obviously cannot forego, are examples of ambiguity, of the interference of two independent sequences of events, to both of which the incident belongs.

Bergson's analysis of the comic discovers in all the variants of comedy of situation, word, or character the central phenomenon, already apparent in comic shapes and motions, of vitality which at the same time makes a somehow mechanical impression. The emphasis lies not so much on the conflict between vitality and stiffness, nor on the forms in which they appear, for example, in individuality vs. type, as on the *contrariety* which, nevertheless, presents itself, and seeks to be accepted as, *unity.* Bergson is able to demonstrate such contrariety in three elementary phenomena which in their obviousness are intelligible even to the child: the jumping jack, the marionette, and the snowball. In all three we see a certain capriciousness and independence, an elasticity, a convincing mobility, an expansive power, all of which are intermingled with an obvious automaticism and mechanism: they can all be regulated and directed. Thus, like the rubber ball and the swing, they entice the child to play. But they are not just playthings; they are funny as well. The snowball is not just a ball, but in rolling over the snow it becomes something else, from which an unexpected effect results: an expansive mechanism of striking disproportionality.

Everything disproportionate—elaborate detours, violent exertions which lead back to the starting point, tensions which dissolve into nothing, gestures and expressive movements which do not conceal their emptiness—all this is overpoweringly funny, for it demonstrates contrariety as unity. And the only question is whether this contrariety between the living and the mechanistic—both taken in their human sense—must be involved, i.e., whether we (and in whatever aspect) must always catch the individual in some kind of inflexibility, or in any case as lapsing into inflexibility, in order to find something funny. If the comic is limited to the sphere of the human, can it be understood as a conjunction of lifelikeness and rigidity? Finally, is the comic essentially social in origin and function?

The limitation of the comic to the human sphere does not imply that we only laugh about human beings or can find only people funny. Bergson himself provides the best counterexamples: a half-clipped dog, a flower bed with artificially colored flowers, a grove in which the trees are plastered with election posters, an artificially regulated waterfall which the observer who has paid his entrance fee can release by pulling a string. But Bergson explains these as examples of disguise: nature appears here as in a mask. In this way, we need not think of nature as actually becoming humanized, but, contrary to her essential character, she wears a garment, she plays a role. She exercises—against her nature and only through human will—a function which we know otherwise only in man.

Nature is unambiguous. She may be strange, uncanny, or violent, but she is what she is: evident and entire. Stones, plants, animals may originate from the plan of providence or from the creative play of blind forces—still, as they happen to be, they have nothing to hide. Neither seed nor husk,* they are everything at once. But there can be cases which do not give this impression. The zoologist will perhaps be less receptive to such feelings than a child or a naïve person who finds the hippopotamus, the sea cow, or the rhinoceros hornbill just as comic as the penguin or the elaborately clipped dog. The penguin and the dog

* Goethe: "Natur hat weder Kern noch Schale."—M. G.

remind us of human beings, but the hippopotamus, the sea cow, and the hornbill have in themselves a comic effect. Why?

Here there is no longer a question of anything human, but these creatures themselves appear as caricatures of animals. Now we carry within ourselves a kind of idea or schema of the animal as such, a schema doubtless conditioned by our range of experience and often unjustified but which is in accord with the most familiar species: not too big, not too fat, not too disproportionate. Snakes and fish, birds and game, lions and whales—to each one its form is suited, and each affects us as being one of the many possibilities in which animal life can take shape. But still there are exceptions which appear as grotesque exaggerations of a form, as nature's jokes (of whose lack of humor only the scientific specialist can convince himself).

Plants and inorganic structures are obviously unable to have comic effects, provided that they do not, like cacti, for instance, or rock and cloud formations, remind us of other structures of a vegetable, animal, or human kind. With regard to plants, stones, mountains, and lakes, our fancy is to some extent free from bias. Such things are growths or pure shapes whose variety can play what games it will. Our idea of a natural growth or form contains no notion of extravagance in the sense of being too thick or too thin, too flat or too round. In this respect immobility may have some significance. Plants, water, clouds, stones are moved but they do not move themselves. Their *habitus* is passive; they give no hint of anything we could call behavior.

Animal *habitus,* on the other hand, is active; animals behave —gracefully or clumsily, impetuously or sluggishly, aggressively or hesitantly. Thus the perspective of a reference to standards creeps into the appearance of animal life. For wherever a mode of behavior confronts us, it presents itself in the light of norms which—like gracefulness, swiftness, aggressiveness—are indeed applicable to men as well but not derived from him. Moreover, it is in behavior that the actual form acquires its distinct outline, its meaningful shape: the gross body appears like a dead weight (even if it really isn't), the hooked beak as the permanent denial of all "natural" proportion between beak, head, and torso. Thus a living creature which exhibits behavior, or acts (and this means in some ways moves "itself"), is more or less in harmony with its body or in opposition to it: it assumes a kind of challenge —to our eyes. And this is all that matters in finding something comic or absurd in form or behavior.

The comic in animals rests, not on more or less conscious analogies to human beings, but on a conflict between an idea or a norm which we apply to the appearance in our imagination (by reason of habit and aesthetic prejudice)—a norm in the light of which the animal form immediately appears to us—*and* the species of animal which actually confronts us. The zoologist tries in vain to enlighten us on this point. For him, there are rarities but nothing funny—no more, for example, than there can be for him disgusting animals. For in nature, in contrast to the human world, everything must be just as it is. And yet as phenomena animals do stand out. To naïve souls they sometimes seem, as blunders of nature, to contradict the norm which tolerantly admits the greatest extremes and yet watches over every form. And so (against all serious teaching), they seem to embody in themselves that typical rivalry between life and mechanism which, in Bergson's view, excites us to laughter.

Precisely as such the comic conflict is *not* confined to the sphere of the human but can break out at any time where an outward appearance offends against a norm which it *nevertheless obviously obeys*. Among animals, this opposition to the norm is only apparent, since our common sense must convince us of the expediency and necessity of their behavior and appearance. They cannot dissemble and disguise themselves; they cannot be other than they are. Thus the apparently comic is nevertheless based on their appearance and is not only a reflection of human analogies. Our biological judgment rightly corrects—or, better, dispels—the comic character of the impression in such cases, but it cannot find fault with the impression itself. This has its own aesthetic truth and its own critical norm. What isn't really comic can really appear so. It does not become more nearly genuine when it enters the human domain. The possibility of being voluntary or involuntary is as little decisive for it as is the degree of adaptation to the norm against which the appearance has rebelled.

Only the effect of the comic, not its essence, is strengthened in the human sphere, since norms can be required of man as a free being capable of responsibility and control. With this requirement he acknowledges a depth in himself, a gap in himself. Out of this depth, he must somehow bridge this gap in order to gain a true relation to things. To the naïve eye this seems to be so in the animal; with man it is really so. Nature has created him as an existence with a double ground, belonging to several levels and aspects, among which his conflicting powers are divided, so that they can occasionally give a comic impression. Against the background of such claims as man advances—to individuality and thus to being unique, unrepeatable, and irreplaceable, to dignity, self-possession, resilience, balance, harmony between body, soul, and mind—practically everything that man is, has, and does can have a comic effect. Resemblance of the kind that makes two men indistinguishable is funny; aping of face, inflection, movements is funny; mistaken identity—is funny. Dressing in costume (and every form of dress which has been long enough out of fashion, but not so long that we no longer identify with it, acts as a costume) is—funny. Disproportionate forms, awkward behavior, excesses of any kind, monomanias, absent-mindedness, rigidities: all are inexhaustible sources of the comic in comparison to the only occasional and inauthentic even though really funny side of animals.

Only man is really comic because he belongs to several levels of existence at once. The entwining of his individual in his social existence, of his moral person in psychophysically conditioned character and type, of his intellect in the body, opens ever and again new chances of collision with some norm or other. On this account, the theory of the comic is always inclined to slight the inauthentically comic aspect of animals and take it as derivative, which it is not. Thus the theory itself perverts its own crucial insight, namely, that in origin and function the comic is of a nonsocial nature, even though it develops to its full richness only within the radius of social existence. What a society finds funny, what it laughs at, changes in the course of history, because it belongs to the change in our consciousness of norms. On the other hand, the comic itself is no social product, and the laughter which responds to it no warning signal, no punishment (which it can become in a society), but an elementary reaction to what is disturbing in the comic conflict. Eccentric to his environment [*Umwelt*], with a prospect on a world [*Welt*], man stands between gravity and levity, between sense and nonsense, and thus before the possibility of their inextricable, ambiguous, contrary relation, which he can do nothing with, from which he must free himself, but which at the same time still holds him bound.

To this extent, then, the comic is to be explained as the occasion of laughter. Again, one encounters in it the initial form of an ambivalence which, to be sure, no longer remains imprisoned in the quality of a titillating stimulus and which has also outgrown the condition of suspense between constraint and caprice characteristic of play. The comic lies wholly on the side of the object, of the situation, of the character of what is given to it (to which I myself belong, if I appear funny to myself). It is a quality of appearance of this given. Admittedly, it appeals not only to our senses but to our apprehension and understanding of conduct, facial expression, bearing, language, attire, and so on, but neither is it ever completely detached from our senses. Comic phenomena, scenes, actions, persons are, as appearances, in themselves ambiguous and paradoxical for our apprehension. They never leave us in peace and yet never offer the prospect that we can "do anything" with them. Yet since the appearance itself—in spite of its "impossibility"—persists, and we can obviously "manage" to live with it, we fall into an ambivalent attitude to it, an attitude which not only comes to no decision between attraction and repulsion, yes and no, and so takes on the character of indecisiveness and doubt; more than that, it rules out a decision altogether and compels us to accept the appearance. We do so; we put up with it, but we leave it to itself: we don't take it seriously.

An ambivalence documented by its own appearance compels us to free ourselves from the comic object, to break off, however we can, the contact of understanding and use and leave the object to its mere appearance. But of what sort is this ambivalence, this double value and double sense? Of what nature is the comic conflict, the comic incongruity?

The Bergsonian answer can be linked to ours insofar as the coexistence of life and mechanism represents an opposition to norms, in which the role of the norm is assigned to life, and its breakdown to mechanism. Opposition to norms (the tasteless, the false, the ugly, the bad) has in itself something offensive and nothing amusing. In order to amuse, this opposition must somehow again be paralyzed. The suppression of the realization of value must at the same time produce and attest the triumph of value. So Bergson also believes. In this way the phenomenon loses its gravity. The contesting and denial of the norm must be overcome; the effect of the conflict must be displayed or at least be obviously provoked in a manifest incongruity.

We may illustrate this relation between norm and factuality, so decisive for the occurrence of the comic effect, by reference to a formulation of F. G. Jünger, taken from his work *Über das Komische*.[14] This is one of the latest studies on the theme and certainly no less penetrating than older and better-known treatments of the subject. According to Jünger, the comic makes its appearance only with reference to a rule with which it clashes. Comic conflict is distinguished from tragic by the inequality of the parties to the strife. If the tragic effect arises from the equality of the opponents and the equilibrium of their powers, so that the outcome of the struggle cannot be established in advance, the comic effect, conversely, thrives on the inequality of the opposing forces. The comedy consists in the fact that, despite the obvious superioriy of his opponent, the obviously inferior generally begins the battle: the overlong nose by which, so to speak, the face is to be guided; the orchestra member who during a concert puts on the airs of a soloist.

It is not enough, in this situation, that the inferior (the nose, the musician) is overcome; he must begin the quarrel. The provocation, and indeed the incongruous provocation which contains a contradiction, belongs to the schema of the comic conflict. Thus from the start conflict appears, not only as hopeless, but as not to be taken seriously. Errors, blunders, confusions, deceptions as sources of the comic reveal most clearly the contradictory quality of the provocation: Don Quixote against the windmills, the person in a hurry searching for his collar button.

Finally, the comic conflict is completed in the reply, in the rejoinder of the superior, which signifies nothing more than the vindication of the rule. Even the mere perception of the incongruous provocation contains it. Beyond this, the rule can manifest itself independently: wittily, paradoxically, ironically, or humorously. But in every case the rejoinder must be appropriate. It must not, for example, answer a mixup with a murder, or deception with death. "The person who picks up a bottle of poison by mistake and dies, the sharpshooter who misses his mark, the man dying of thirst in the desert who keeps going round in circles: these are cases in which the comic cannot appear because the rejoinder is too strong, and because so strong a reaction does not stand in an aesthetically appropriate relation to the weak provocation." It is not the degree of injury which is decisive but the appropriateness of the reply to the provocation—in itself inappropriate. There are even cases in which one can die a comic death.

The comic provocation is nothing unless it is understood.

The phenomenon reaches completion only in the reply to the phenomenon of a challenge on the part of an inferior, a challenge which is contradictory in itself and not to be taken seriously (even though occasionally intended in all earnest). Herein lies—and this is perhaps the best thing about Jünger's schema of the comic conflict—the reason for the fact that the comic effect is fully developed only in society. The observer here is not the mere eye which takes in finished pictures, but the standard and the rule, the objectification of the norm, in the light of which alone the distorted appears distorted, the crooked, crooked. The comic need not therefore depend upon a group of people; I am also my own observer. But the play of the nonserious conflict unfolds only in the reflection of the norm, which cannot let its light fall on the phenomenon if no mirror is there to reflect it. And since our preoccupation with ourselves and our own concerns is in the first instance too great for us to have an eye for ourselves, the comedy of this preoccupation and the world's appears only to the disinterested observer, the laughing third party —who may even on occasion laugh amid his tears.

Perhaps Jünger's formulation pays too much attention to the balance or imbalance of power, as the Germans of his time were inclined to do. But essentially, all descriptions of an aesthetic state of affairs must be indirectly and metaphorically understood. They can capture it only ephemerally, only so long as the words and the perspective are not exhausted. Its structure must be rediscovered again and again. If there were an adequate and exhaustive conceptual expression for the ambivalence of the comic, it would be robbed of its essence and we of the possibility of a rejoinder. What is laughable is so only because we can't cope with it. A theory which purports to cope with the comic better than we can would have smothered the phenomenon with a concept.

Still, a theory must strive for precision. To the person who has a sense for it, the shocking, disturbing contrariety of the comic is highly unequivocal and definite. To deal with the comic by not taking it seriously is not to be unrelated to it. The only possible relation to the comic *is* not to take it seriously. But the necessity of this attitude can be understood only with reference to its unmanageability by any other means, in accordance with the contrariety inherent in the structure of comic situations. To this extent "comic" means: falling outside the frame of reference, shocking, contradictory, ambiguous—something one can't get hold of and can't set to rights. For this reason, stupidity inclines us to laughter much more than intelligence. The narrower the horizon, the poorer the possibilities of understanding, the quicker do we reach the boundary of senselessness and ambivalence.

Nevertheless man experiences this boundary not only subjectively as his inability to cope with a thing but at the same time as the structure of the thing itself, which prevents his coping with it. In the obvious triumph of being over clarity which the comic appearance directly proclaims, we see revealed its extravagance, its superabundance, its self-derailment—in short, the "out-of-bounds" characteristic of funny things. And it is a counterpoise to the stupidity which too easily finds everything funny that a keen intelligence can strike the same balance from a broad horizon. Such an intelligence need only take care that laughter is not lost in the course of this truly double-entry bookkeeping.

Thus humor as the gift of keeping our sense of the comic must not be taken unilaterally and linked either with emotion or the understanding. Response to the comic comes from the whole man. If we speak of contradiction, ambiguity, and double meaning, indeed, of a contradiction resolving itself in the appearance, still this contradiction does not lie in the rational sphere: it only shines into it from without. If we define the comic as the relation of an inappropriate provocation which proceeds from an inferior, we do indeed invoke the norm. But it would be mistaken to presume to determine once and for all the radius to which the norm belongs. The comic is not a logical, an ethical, or (in the narrower sense) an aesthetic conflict; it has nothing to do with the alternatives true or false, good or evil, beautiful or ugly. They can appear in it, but it is not exhausted by them.

Comedy belongs to the level to which all special applications of norms refer: the level in which man asserts himself as such and as a whole in the world and over against the world. His stance in it somewhere-sometime, i.e., his eccentric position, enables him to accept himself and his world, in which he is at home and knows his way around, as simultaneously circumscribed and open, familiar and strange, replete with sense and nonsense.

In this conjunction lies the core of comedy, but the normal course of life and its duties lets us forget it. We take things in this or that respect and seal them up against ambiguity. But our technique of taking the world seriously and binding it to us, actively and contemplatively, rationally and emotionally, has gaps, in the particular as in the whole. Things surprise us by their appearance, they take an unforeseen turn, they create situations to which we can no longer find a serious response. If such surprises and limiting conditions of our orientation to the world entail on the whole no peril for us, or if we have the power to answer such peril by keeping the freedom of distance, then—always supposing that the phenomenon fulfills the necessary conditions—we find these surprises and situations—funny.

All this may not bring to consciousness the unfathomable nature of the comic as such. Yet, despite this, it makes itself felt and reminds us even in its most insignificant expression of our eccentric position. The art of the great comic, of the caricaturist, the poet, the actor, the clown, knows this and extracts from it the really striking, truly inexorable effects, which gain in illuminating power the nearer they come to the darkness of the tragic.

4. Wit and Humor (The Joke)

Wit, understood not as the talent, impetuous, vigorous, and original, of making a judgment and giving it expression in a striking way (all of which suggests concepts like mother wit, quick-wittedness, and like expressions, often of an old-fashioned kind), but as a form of expression, is frequently interpreted as a subclass of the comic. Kuno Fischer, for example, defines it as "a kind of imagination [*Vorstellungsart*] which is inherent in the creative and communicative power of the comic." Obviously influential here is the clear reference to the laughter which responds to a joke, the enlivening effect which proceeds from it and which it serves, and finally a certain kinship to the structure of the comic, its ambiguity and contrariety. This point, namely, that wit is a form of expression, or at least depends on expression, cannot be seriously disputed. Phrases such as "a prank of history," or the statement that this man, that meeting, deed, or accomplishment is "a complete joke," are clearly to be recognized as metaphorical expressions. More difficult to answer is the question whether wit or joking as such depends on verbal expression. We speak, for example, of a facetious quality in painting, instrumentation, or even in things and situations. Transitions to the ingenious, fanciful, piquant, lively, ticklish, comic, and startling are not always easy to make.

On this account, it is more correct to consider on principle the peculiar character of verbal expression and to ask oneself the question, what specific comic effects can be extracted from it over and above the comic effect as such. We are then led automatically to the joke.

It is "comic," as Bergson said, when a person falls into the snares of language and thus trips over his own legs, so to speak. An unforgettable comedian like Max Pallenberg derived his most effective results from this technique. In the flow of speech, its more or less physical exterior suddenly stands out. We chew over the words, play with them as with foreign bodies: the phenomenon of the comic combat is present. To this same sphere belong the comic confusion of foreign words, the comedy of a pronounced dialect and of stuttering. It is now the articulation and sentence order, now the sound of the words themselves, now their meaning, now the act of speaking that has a comic effect. But in every case, it remains comic.

Jokes that rely on sound and word, on the other hand, however silly, obey another principle. In the answer "Herrings" to the question "What rings are not round?" the aural similarity, without regard for verbal unity and meaning, is made the basis for classifying something under the genus *ring,* by analogy with a procedure for dealing with word forms which in many cases is legitimate. The joke is flat, not because its point ("a formation with the end syllable *-ring* indicates membership in the genus *ring*") turns on the surface similarity of the sound, but because it says nothing by this means. But with such techniques it is also possible to express something significant ("Her ante-Semitism was familiar to me, but her anti-Semitism is something new"). If the point rests on the ambiguity of an expression, as in puns, then in some circumstances a standard joke makes its appearance. For example, with reference to the confiscation of the possessions of the house of Orléans, which was one of the first acts of Napoleon as regent: "C'est le premier vol (flight and robbery) de l'aigle."

Ambiguity as the plurality of meanings, which includes antithesis or contradiction, is frequently the goal of the technique of condensation [*Verdichtung*], as Freud called it. The bowdlerization of words, artificial word formations, and splitting a word into its constituent parts of wordlike character are modes of this technique: Leopold of Belgium, the friend of Cléo de Mérode, as

"Cleopold"; Rothschild, vis-à-vis his chiropodist, as the "famillionaire"; Berlin's judgment of an ultramodern production of *Antigone* as "antique-oh-nay." The joke of such word formations lies in the successful association of a highly suggestive meaning with the empty externality of mere similarity in sound. In the case of *Antigone,* the judgment of the performance was concealed by being present in the pronunciation of the name. In the other cases, words which are not really words say more, through an association of the intended names or properties that is at the same time symbolic, than genuine words could do. Two birds are killed with one stone—which is really no stone at all.

Although, in the examples mentioned above, the amusing effect rests equally on the sound formation and the verbal façade of the linguistic expression, we must not overlook the wittiness of the actual disposition of the words. In this, it is not the comic principle which governs but a unique counterpart which can be characterized as *pointedness.* The comic as such, regardless of whether it is shallow or deep, has no point. It lacks a pivot or center from which the amusing effect proceeds, even if it occurs in the sphere of verbal meaning. Mistakes in the use of foreign words have comic effects when similarity of sound together with an extreme difference in meaning provides occasion for confusion ("republic" for "rubric"). But in principle the same state of affairs occurs if one pronounces any foreign word incorrectly. But as soon as the absurd pronunciation or confusion in its turn makes sense (for instance, instead of *maîtresse,* "mattress"), then our delight at an unintentional and, in the particular case, erotically suggestive witticism coincides with our pleasure at the unintentionally comic.

Pointedness of the facetious does not imply pointedness of expressional nuance. I once had to examine a Cologne student on Kant's categorical imperative. Nothing could be got out of him but the laborious spelling-out of the formulae he had drilled into his head. He had nothing to say in reply to even the most general questions about the nature, significance, and basic perspective of this ethic. Finally, in order to bring home to him the urgency and the radical nature of the imperative, I asked: "Well, what do you think of such an ethic, of rigorous fulfillment of duty?" His answer: "Gee, I've always got on pretty well with it." Here the overwhelming dimension of the incongruity, supported by the comfortably indifferent Cologne intonation, comes to light in the modestly complacent remark with which an ethic that rejects nothing more vigorously than the standard of success is accepted in the light of that very standard. And then, to cap it all, to do this, not through and through (as would have been, temperamentally at least, in accord with the rigorously categorical), but by a personally mild weighing of the matter, as if an ethic were an advertising slogan, a brand of cigars, or a patent medicine.

All the conditions for a joke are at hand. All that is missing in the candidate's answer is the pointed expression of the way in which it actually "displaces" the meaning of the question. This displacement is facetious in the highest degree, although it doesn't work by means of a verbal formulation. Like the self-contradiction contained in assessing the ethic of duty in the light of personal self-satisfaction, the displacement too remains unspoken in the answer. Its treasure of allusions to human dispositions (the sure instinct of the Rhinelander, his habit of weighing one thing against another—coming as he does from a long tradition that has never been established on explicit principles, against the rigor of Prussian deontologism with its Königsberg stamp) gives this anecdote its particular human cast. It effects a reconciliation of the displacement of meaning with the self-contradiction contained in the response, although the respondent makes no reference to this.

Our analysis teaches us the following: A remark can be ever so funny in content, form, and situation—yet if certain conditions are not fulfilled through which the point can be expressed, the remark is not a joke. These conditions are not dependent on the verbal apprehension of the surface meaning, or double meaning, of a remark, or on the opinion of the speaker, but on the import of the remark, through which it makes its point.

Our analysis of such remarks may hide this truth; for, in interpreting their meaning—whether understood as open or concealed, direct or indirect, explicit or allusive—we may be driven to substitute for it one or more *judgments* to which, as far as content goes, the meaning in question is equivalent. We introduce judgments into our analysis to clarify the puzzling remark and to bring into view the complication of meaning.

In this way an interpretation inadvertently turns into an interpolation, an exposition of meaning as the vehicle of a comic, facetious quality and amusing effect becomes a translation into the language of serious statements, synonymous with the original. In the belief that, with such judgmental expressions, it has formulated not only the serious equivalent of the amusing remark but also its true meaning, such analysis, focused on the logical structure of its result, arrives at the conviction that joking and repartee are judgments or convey judgments. In Hochfeld's formulation,[15] for example, this conviction appears as follows: "The joke is a proposition which, on the basis of the ambiguity of a word, asserts simultaneously two judgments which have nothing but their phonetic configuration in common, but in such a way that one judgment is presented openly and the second in concealment. The effect of every joke depends on the unexpected discovery of the concealed meaning; ultimately, on the fact that our language, stemming as it does from the prescientific consciousness of man, is not unequivocal in its vocabulary and idiomatic usage." Our example completely disproves this theory.

The Berlin zoo visitor looks at a giraffe and remarks: "What a gullet, what a guzzle!" Where are the two judgments hiding that have nothing in common but their phonetic form? The facetious compactness which passes over not only judgments but a whole train of thought (the nub of which is: the longer the neck, the longer the enjoyment), by uttering, like a deep sigh, a maximum of (unrealizable) desire in a minimum of expression—on the basis of a thought as surprisingly obvious as it is debatable—such compactness rests on a silent ambiguity. In the "explanation" it must naturally be expressed, but the remark itself does not contain it, it only intimates it. In order to make it intelligible, i.e., to transpose it into the language of serious judgments, the ambiguity of the word "long" must be exhibited in two judgments, one of which is presented openly, the other as concealed. At this point, theory overreaches the phenomenon.

To intimate by allusion in virtue of a multiplicity of meaning which can be reached in very different ways is the true art, the inner form, of wit. To speak silently, yet so that the silent message is not left to the whim of the speaker or hearer but delivered over to the remark itself: by means of equivocation, by displacement in the answer to a question (which only suggests the double meaning), by omission of connecting trains of thought, by paradoxes—that is the function of every point. In the point we can grasp radically the origin of the amusing effect, in contrast to the comic, which lays hold of us without our being able to say why. But at the same time the axis and pivot elude the direct grasp of insight. Only the meaning that becomes translucent and transpicuous in *another* medium has a facetious effect. If the indirectness is transformed into directness and the meaning of the remark into indicative judgments, then the effect vanishes.

Hence the venerable insight that brevity is the soul of wit, that it lies in an unexpected idea, in lightning-like illumination, in a surprising discovery, in the abrupt association of two incongruent elements. Hence also the talk of incongruity between concept and perception which is said to be bridged by the joke. We find it, for example, in Schopenhauer's formulation: wit is a paradoxical subsumption of a phenomenon under a heterogeneous concept, a subsumption which, however, has a certain semblance of reality and justification. Hence, finally, his description of the joke as a playful judgment which brings apparently incompatible things into unexpected relation: "Der verkleidete Priester, der jedes Paar kopuliert . . . mit verschiedenen Trauformeln" (Jean Paul): in German *kopulieren* means both "to couple" and "to copulate"; so here: "The pretended priest, who couples differently with every couple he couples."

Tension which dissolves pleasurably into nothing (a logical nothing), lightning surprise, brevity in the temporal and formal sense, the momentary appearance of an objective coherence which doesn't stand up to a direct inspection of the actual state of affairs—all such definitions are, like the judgments called in to serve the function of the analysis of the joke, equivalents of the double meaning that has been playfully suggested. While the use of double meaning in itself need no more produce a joke than does a mere allusion, allusion through ambiguity does fulfill the conditions of the joke. It derives its impact from the concealment or disclosure, as the case may be, of the other meaning, its depth from the import of the anecdote to which this process leads us.

To allude to something, to hint of it, to speak figuratively, to intimate, to suggest, is possible linguistically in very different ways, depending on the circumstances. In serious situations allusion will not make use of double meanings except where it belongs to the style of utterance, as, for example, in the practice of the Greek oracles. It is possible to hint at something by association, by awakening memories, suggesting thoughts, arousing wishes, and in every case this means only the disclosure of a deeper, different direction of understanding which had not been explicitly indicated. Again, double meaning implies using the same expression to suggest two different things. The use of the expression usually excludes one meaning. But if one manages to retain the double meaning, then one can hint playfully at something unsaid. One way to do this, though by no means the only one, is to use a word or phrase with a double meaning. Here the point of the joke is born: word-play in the true sense. But the point can be—and in the more enigmatic jokes usually is—given in disguise and indirectly, without itself being presented in a particular expression. The omission of words, leaving blanks, self-contradictions, and inclusion of the situation in which the remark stands: all these are tools in trade for making a point.

To find a verbal form in which to intimate something silently means to speak wittily. Hence the amusing effect cannot be reduced to a contemplated absurdity, to a playing with nonsense, or to an illogicality that was meant to be thought clever. All such definitions are too narrow and fit only certain categories of wit and humor. Nonsense and absurdity can be communicated just as easily as meaningful errors or truths. The paradoxical can take the form of wit, but wit neither necessarily coincides with the paradoxical nor is it bound to paradox. Only in the overlay of several meanings, i.e., through the possibility of being guided in more than one direction by verbal expression, do we arrive at the joke. This tells us nothing about the relation of the upper to the lower meaning nor about the funniness of the expression. It is the overlay and intersection that are essential, and the *place* of intersection is what we understand as the point. We grasp it, not, indeed, for itself, but in the *achievement* of transparency of meaning, in the meaning, in flight, so to speak, as it grips us as change of direction, surprise, leaping spark, lightning illumination, and shock.

Reimann's epigram: "Germany is a Columbus egg. One need only push it to the end * and it will surely be able to ride by it-

* The joke discussed in this paragraph depends on a verbal ambiguity and an incongruity of images, neither of which will be obvious to the English-speaking reader. *Auf die Spitze treiben* means both literally "to push to the end" (or, as we would say of the famous egg, "push down on the end") and "to drive to extremes." The reference to the egg's riding suggests, as Plessner explains, Bismarck's remark about being firmly in the saddle, so that the German reader

self!" contains in its mid-part the equivocal phrase which joins onto the initial passage in the literal sense and at the same time lets us divine the other sense, namely, provoking Germany to a crisis. By this means tension is created: Germany is a problem which no one can manage but for which there is an ingeniously simple solution, a solution in Columbus' sense, in the sense of extremism. The tension demands resolution, its intensification demands a *coup de théâtre*. Instead of this (in veiled sarcasm directed to the lack of principle characterizing the politics of catastrophe which abandons a land to its fate, with an ironic bow to Bismarck's saying about being firmly in the saddle—a pronouncement which history has bitterly refuted) the imaginative, doubly impossible prospect, which allows the tension to dwindle to nothing. A twofold point: represented once in the double meaning of the phrase "push it to the end," and then not strictly "represented" but effective in the disruption of the image by a quotation which fits like a fist in the eye, like the egg on the horse—and which suggests the futility of going to extremes, of the inspired solution, by an outlandish application of Bismarck's pronouncement.

In a particular case it may be difficult to reach agreement as to whether a facetious remark falls into the *literary* category of the joke.[16] The oracular sayings, riddles, and proverbs already mentioned work with the same conditions of concealed ambiguity, the overlaying and intersection of meanings. In contrast to such forms, we can differentiate the joke as a remark suitable to an occasion, which is confined neither to an interrogatory form nor to the expression of a general experience of life. Facetiousness [*Witzigkeit*], on the other hand, is a type and manner of speaking which unmistakably has a wider compass than "the joke" as a literary form. By means of the intersection of meanings it achieves the amusing relaxation of tension.

In the developed sense of the word, "wit" or "joke" stands here as the representative of facetiousness when it is a matter of ascertaining the reason for the amusing effect (discharged as laughter). Especially in our context this difference in the aesthetics of speech may be ignored. For we have all along been

---

finds the stern Iron Chancellor suddenly transformed into the ludicrous figure of an equestrian Humpty Dumpty.—M. G.

This passage in the third edition, beginning "Reimanns Prägung," p. 132, is corrupt. I have taken the correct version from the first edition.—J. S. C.

seeking the laughable effects which can be extracted from language over and above its comic appeal. It is certainly not only the wag and the teller of funny stories who have the ability to manage a witty discourse; so has anyone who has at his command allusion and pithy formulation.

But why does facetiousness have an amusing effect? Why does it make us laugh? By reference to a general criterion like ambiguity, double meaning, or ambivalence little has been gained. To be sure, such a rule gives us a hint of the relation to the comic, to play, even to tickling, and finds the levity of the situation in the lack of univocality in what is said, which is to be understood, not as a vagueness but as *double-entendre* in the strict sense of the term. But since the particular power of the joke consists in putting several meanings together in such a way that (figuratively speaking) they are overlaid and do *not* expel one another, since they are held together by an expression of special significance, it is precisely by means of the joke that language exceeds its limit. A mode of understanding tied and directed to an expression becomes independent *of* it *by* that very tie and direction.

This discovery, which we make afresh with every amusing phrase or remark, is something which takes us by surprise and reveals our double relation to language: that we speak in it and against it. What a person can clarify to himself in the abstract and what he has to deal with in every possible way in practice —namely, that in the sense of a complete congruence between form and content there is the "right" expression *and* yet, on the other hand, that no expression fits, that an unbridgeable gap between word and fact makes the word dispensable—this is what the joke confirms in concrete unity. But in contrast to what is just comic in speech, the *joke* operates not on the level of language (speech, pronunciation, etc.) by means of slips of the tongue, malapropisms, stuttering, dialect, but on the level of talk (relations of meaning) through the agency of the intersection of meanings.

By way of parenthesis: The possibility of amusing expression in images and gestures also rests on this double relation to language. The character of the meaning conveyed by them is not significantly changed when a sign, musical phrase, or any bodily gesture is chosen instead of a word or sentence. For this reason, the dispute over the question of whether or not joking is bound to language is not to be decided with reference to joking in pictures, musical phrases, or physical gestures alone. It is not the means of expression which is decisive but the mode of expressive meaning communicated by it, and this is essentially linguistic meaning or, to put it plainly, the meaning of discourse, which can also be put in words and sentences. Joking is bound to discourse and develops only in and through meanings whose communication and understanding require either language or substitutes for language such as pictures, musical phrases, or gestures. On the other hand, joking is not tied to words, let alone judgments.

Yet this does not blur the boundaries of the comic. An example: [17] The American congressional elections are about to take place. In the forthcoming contest, the Republican National Committee expects much from a symbolic emblem which exhibits an impetuous, onrushing force. Now, the traditional party emblem is an elephant, which embodies steadiness and power, solidity and ponderosity, gravity and repose. Resolved: A new emblem in which the elephant, in wild movement, seems to be filled with elemental vehemence. "A wag changed this heroic image into its opposite by means of a small addition. He placed a bee on the good old elephant's tail which plagues him so much with the poison of the New Deal that he frantically takes flight."

Granted that an elephant brought into wild motion by a bee sting can produce a comical effect through the incongruity of cause and effect. But in this case, we laugh not about this, but about the clever shift of meaning of the image to its opposite—a shift which cannot be understood from the picture alone, even though it can give its message without a long caption. But we must know what the elephant signifies, we must be familiar with the situation, in order to grasp the meaning, which in this case makes use of a wordless, but therefore all the more pregnant, language. A comic impression, on the other hand, requires no explanation. It "speaks" through itself, i.e., it intimates nothing.

After this digression, we return to our original question: Why does facetiousness have an amusing effect? Why does it make us laugh? As we know, it is the device of the intersection of meanings that gives the answer. It is from such intersection that the amusing effect must proceed. At first sight, it seems natural to explain double meaning as a special form of the comic, but our spontaneous feeling that the comic is surely different from the witty already resists such a notion. The pointedness and pregnancy of several meanings contrasted to one another and yet posited as one are unmistakable indications of such a difference.

This is why the joke has been presented as a kind of play (and it has proved tempting to see a play on words in every joke). The expedient of making wit a play of thought or a playful judgment [18] does not take us very far, since many "plays" of or with thought are anything but witty. (And even if they are, then *why*?) But even apart from all this, the play-character of joking still remains questionable. We do not oscillate to and fro between mutually veiled meanings, nor can we recognize in their unexpected disclosure a constantly recurring moment of tension which entices us to repetition. On the contrary, a joke forfeits the greater part of its amusing effect (not its quality) when we are already familiar with it. At the same time, if one takes the concept of play in the breadth of the Kant-Schiller aesthetic, then it vanishes when we apply it to the limited category of the joke and of repartee. This concept then implies no more and no less than lack of seriousness, and so, indeed, fits the character of the aesthetic sphere as a whole (in the sense that life is serious while art is joyous). But it misses the restricted sphere of the amusing as such.

Finally, there remains only the phenomenon of titillation, to which some believe the joke must be reduced if we are to understand its entertaining effect. The judgment theory of the joke, strange to say, supports this far-fetched idea. For this theory would define it as the paradoxical subsumption of a phenomenon under a heterogeneous concept with a certain semblance of justification (Schopenhauer), as the association of remotely related ideas in the sense of the Kantian formula: "The joke pairs heterogeneous notions which often lie far apart in terms of the laws of imagination, and is a unique faculty of producing similarities which belongs to the understanding insofar as it brings objects under genera." This interpretation (also advocated by Jean Paul Vischer and by many idealists) lays stress upon the combination of concepts and elements which really have nothing in common but only appear to have. It therefore associates with this self-conflicting combination a psychical state in which pleasure and displeasure are in conflict with each other. Thus Hecker (*loc. cit.*) formulates this thought: "In the joke, it is a matter of two ideas whose incompatibility, and yet possible compatibility, with each other form the source of pleasure and displeasure." From here it is only a step to recognizing, in this conflict that forces us to laugh, the same functional mechanism which rules in the ambivalent excitation of titillation. But, in fact, the point at issue is neither conflict nor displeasure, and the joke cannot be understood, even in a figurative sense, as an exalted mental titillation.

So the question of the joke as a source of amusement seems to be driven back to its exclusive properties, which serve the intersection of meanings: the technique of expression through concealment and silent intimation, and surprise. They cannot be separated. Granted, someone occasionally tries to reduce the amusing effect to the shock alone. We know those cases where we are alarmed by something and then break out in relieved laughter as soon as we see that "it was nothing." Kant's other formulation of the joke as an expectation which dwindles to nothing seems to be confirmed by such experiences.

But clearly (even in cunningly contrived presentation) joking lacks the decisive ability to shock. It is precisely on those occasions when the hearer is put in suspense—although this applies by no means to all jokes, let alone for the understanding of wit in general—that he expects a joke. But whether we are surprised or expect a surprise makes a decisive difference for the psychological dynamics of the process. In the first case, the shock results from the complete unexpectedness with which something strikes us, and the laughter results from the disproportion between the depth of the alarm and the harmlessness, indeed, the obviousness, of its cause. (In this case, moreover, both sides of the transition are to be taken into account: the strength of the emotion which strives for discharge in its dynamic disproportion to the cause *and* the comedy of the disproportion in our behavior, at which we laugh when it is over.) In the second case, since we expect a surprise, the shock will be too slight to evoke a strong outburst, and our behavior remains restrained.

In contrast to such one-sided views, Freud's theory [19] adheres to the goal of understanding the amusing effect by taking the joke as a *unity of expressive form and content.* To be sure, its basic conception seems to us to miscarry, but the direction in which it looks for a solution is not affected by this error. For Freud, humor, comedy, wit are sources of pleasure because they save man's psychic expenditure. Usually our social upbringing imposes on us inhibitions, confinements, and repressions. If we are spared these, then we feel that we have been relieved of a burden. Thus, buried sources of pleasure from a time of life in which we reacted psychically with a lesser expenditure of energy, our childhood, are once again set free. Humor arouses pleasure because it spares us expenditure of feeling; comedy, because it spares us expenditure in ideas; joking, because it spares us expenditure in inhibition.

The joke attains its goal of economy chiefly through the technique of expression. The brevity essential to it means economy in words. Typical examples of its expression are condensation, displacement or reversal, consolidation (by turning the repulse in the direction of the attack), representation by the contrary (related to irony), especially popular in the form of one-up-manship,* and finally allusion. (The progress in method of classification as compared with earlier divisions in terms of homonyms, puns, intellectual jokes, nonsense jokes, etc., is clear. Freud sees the natural basis of systematization in the point of the joke.)

But pleasure in joking belongs not only to technique, but just as much to intention or even bias.† Harmless jokes without bias which delight merely through their technique—Freud cites the spoonerism here, in which pleasure at recovery of the familiar provides the decisive turn—evoke only weak feeling. On the other hand, the tendentious joke—the malicious and the obscene—calls forth true outbursts of liberated and liberating laughter. Here the joke is an outlet to freedom. It bypasses inhibition and creates the possibility of making the object of our hatred laughable, or the impropriety which we dare not mention obscurely visible.

The attainment of pleasure through a tendentious joke results from the sudden fulfillment of a drive that had hitherto been inhibited. The awakening as well as the maintenance of psychic inhibition requires the expenditure of psychic energy. If this inhibition is broken through or circumvented, then the energy which would otherwise have been expended becomes free and is discharged as laughter: the gain in pleasure matches the saving of energy or inhibition. This saving of the energy of inhibition or repression is the source of the pleasurable relief we feel at a tendentious joke. In a harmless joke the short-circuiting of the expressive technique as such gives us enjoyment, for it

* *Überbietung,* literally, "outdoing."—M. G.

† Literally, *Tendenz:* "tendency."—M. G.

saves us troublesome conceptual labor, it enables us to play, and to have our way, as freely with nonsense as with sense.

Thus, Freud believes, pleasure in the joke may be traced back—via technique and bias—to the relief of an already existing compulsion or of an expenditure of energy still to be performed. But this relief occurs only when the energy released by the removal of the inhibition breaks through as laughter. By itself the saving in energy does not have this result. On this account, the joke develops its liberating effect only in communication. Thus maker and hearer obtain objective certainty that the arrow has hit its mark. In laughter they assure themselves of their regained freedom.

Finally, the joke liberates under a general condition. If it is to overcome unconscious inhibitions, it must not arise from conscious deliberation and artificial contrivance. It must itself be the product of the unconscious, born from the sudden flash of thought, if it is to have its effect as convincing, pertinent, and a means of liberation.

Joking reveals this origin through its kinship with dreams. The task of dreaming is to break through the inhibitions of consciousness. Repressed thoughts and desires, our latent dream-thoughts, are transformed by the activity of dreaming * into the content of the dream. Dream-work shapes the latent dream-thoughts through condensation and compression in images, through displacement from the subconscious into consciousness, and thence, retroactively influencing the subconscious, through indirect representation. Now the techniques of joking are the same as those of dreams. The specific brevity of the joke thus no longer appears as merely the consequence of the tendency to economize but, over and above this, as the result of unconscious processing.

Dreams and joking let us recover buried sources of pleasure because they bridge the abyss between consciousness and the unconscious. But while with dreams the displacement can be so great that we fail to understand them in conscious thought, joking, to be effective, must contain the conditions of intelligibility. The dream, a disguised wish, related to our most personal life-interests, is an asocial product directed to the saving of displeasure. The joke, on the other hand, is a social product and represents an instrument for winning back lost sources of

* *Traumarbeit:* "dream-work."—M. G.

pleasure within sociey—be it noted, a society of adults. On this account, the naïve is also closely related to joking in Freud's view, because it appears to skip over inhibitions which are present in the observer. The correspondence of wit and naïve utterance can extend even to the technical means of expression, such as similarity of sound, misuse of words, and so on. In some measure, the phenomenon of the naïve forms a transition from the comic as something we hit upon unintentionally and wit.

Relative to earlier explanations, Freud's theory also signifies an essential advance, insofar as it makes laughter intelligible on the basis of the structure of the joke. To be sure, it does not go so far as to ask why the liberated excess of energy is released precisely as laughter (it does not put the question at all, since the problem lies outside its sphere of interest). Yet it does indicate a reason why the amusement of a joke brings a real relief, a sudden gain in energy which has pleasant, eruptive, and, at the same time, recuperative effect. This gain is supposed to result from a saving in the energy of inhibition which is unconsciously achieved. The explanation may be plausible for tendentious jokes. For harmless jokes, however, which Freud himself has said need not in any sense be without content or of less value than the tendentious, the explanation seems forced. Brevity, as economy in words, will ordinarily require increased expenditure of energy, increased intensity in comprehension, attention, insight, and liveliness of imagination for the joker as well as for his listeners. The elaboration of arguments according to logical rules and precise, careful reasoning saves in mental energy by comparison with a lightning-like flash of insight, which is more demanding and hence also has a smaller public. If, in general, one operates with the idea of economy (which in psychological matters is highly problematical), then Freud's calculation is in error here.

Brevity is a demand on the power of comprehension, hence an inhibition and psychic damming which the listener must overcome. It is the technique of covert camouflage, and of the sly bewitchment of meaning, that *creates* the very resistance whose *collapse* it at the same time produces. In this the joke is related to the riddle, except that it usually foregoes the interrogative form in order to attain a purer overlay of meanings. But if one has really grasped the expressive technique of the joke and of repartee as a means of relieving inhibition, then one need not appeal to unconscious inhibitions in order to explain the pleasurable gain in liberated surplus energy that accrues when they are broken through. In this case, the pleasurable excess, the sudden relief, results from the double play of creating a difficulty which overcomes itself. Naturally, tendencies which are unrealized in a given society for moral, political, or other reasons can make use of this double play, and the eruptive quality of laughter shows that in such cases a special latent tension is also involved. Hence both the joke as such and its effect cannot be understood only through an unconscious mechanism or according to a principle of economy.

Nor is the Freudian standpoint exhaustive with respect to the motives of joking and wit. Wit can come simply from delight in agility and indirection, in the play of inhibition and its dissolution. It can also serve hostile and obscene impulses. Not less frequently, however, it is a means of freeing ourselves from our emotions, concealing them, or at least acting as if we were their masters. As a way of talking about things which are too difficult and too delicate to allude to seriously, it will often be bitter, sarcastic, caustic, cynical, multifariously ironic, but rarely humorous and relaxed. For this kind of wit, Nietzsche's word holds good: The joke is the epigram on the death of a feeling. To which we add: An epigram that hits its coffin nail on the head.[20]

Thus if the *depth* of the effect of a joke depends on the strength and character of the tension that stands behind it, the amusing effect likewise rests on the witty technique of the veiled transformation and sly interweaving of meanings which creates an inhibition by the same means with which it overcomes it. In this lies the frivolity of the joke. If we want to speak here of paradox or self-contradiction, then these concepts must be related to the function of repartee and not to the particular meanings that happen to be involved. The tension dammed up by the inhibition is released in grasping the point of the joke and drains off in laughter.

But why is it precisely laughter which brings about this easing of tension? This question still remains to be elucidated.

5. Embarrassment and Despair

As the final class of occasions of laughter, we turn to situations involving embarrassment and despair. It is no accident that the analysis of the causes of laughter usually ignores these. In these cases laughter lacks its unequivocally liberating character, its character of relaxed good cheer. It sounds choked, and the embarrassed or despairing person has the feeling of a misplaced expression. Besides, in embarrassment we easily become conscious of the comedy of the situation, especially in the eyes of others, so that our own state is concealed from us and we laugh at this funny situation, not out of embarrassment.

This sudden change is natural in just those situations in which the person no longer knows what to do, either with himself or with the world, in which he is at his wit's end and finds himself in a vacuum, standing before a blank wall or at the edge of an abyss. He is thrown back upon himself and experiences a most painful pause, a break in his ordinary existence which reveals to him a disproportion between himself and his environment. A disproportion that can be the source of his need and at the same time of its alleviation: enchainment and liberation in one, *if* he allows himself to be seized by the humor of his orientation. This flight into the comic explains in good part why we laugh in embarrassment (and despair). But at the same time there is still genuine embarrassed or desperate laughter.

We can be *helpless* in relation to things, tasks, other people, or situations. We are *embarrassed* before people by whom we believe ourselves observed or unmasked. We don't know how to behave, can take no stand on the situation, and thus feel ourselves in a state of involuntary isolation. We would like to find the right point of departure but see ourselves hemmed in. Typical for many people—especially clumsy individuals and above all children and adolescents—is the embarrassment they feel on joining a social gathering. The knowledge that they are observed makes them embarrassed. The knowledge or belief that many eyes are directed on them makes them insecure. One sees oneself as a picture, i.e., taken on the strength of the kind of figure he cuts. This insecurity is raised to the level of embarrassment if its knowledge or supposed knowledge blocks whatever relation of the person to his body would be correct for the execution of the behavior required. He then finds no words, stutters, stammers, or stands as if rooted to the spot.

Being observed and believing oneself to be taken as a figure of fun, however, is only one source of embarrassment. Imagining that one has been seen through and sized up has a more intensive effect. Thus even the hardened individual will be seized by embarrassment and confusion if he is up against a man of acute judgment, above all in an encounter on which a great deal depends. In every case, the embarrassed individual fancies himself objectified and, as it were, "undressed." This does not apply to cases of embarrassment involving the consciousness of an unbridgeable distance from one's companion or of an inability to find the right tone—something which, on occasion, can as easily happen to adults vis-à-vis children as to pupils with their partners in a dancing class.

In any event, the embarrassed person is ashamed of his embarrassment, which betrays an exaggerated attachment to the self, consciousness of inferiority, ambition, and vanity. But embarrassment as such has nothing to do with shame. Under certain circumstances, embarrassment arises from a pronounced modesty and sensitivity, but it is still not to be mistaken for shame.[21] One can be ashamed of oneself for any reason, a state of affairs, a failure, and this consciousness is not bound to society. Embarrassment, on the other hand, is the incapacity to cope with a situation that is determined by some social encounter. As opposed to simple disorientation, however, one reviews the situation only too well, or believes that he does so, and thus becomes conscious of a disproportion between his review and understanding of what the situation requires and his inability to measure up to these requirements. Animals are spared this consciousness of a fateful intersection between the situation one is in and the situation one controls. For they have no consciousness of standing anywhere at all. They can, indeed, be seriously disoriented and confused; they can also doubt and fall into uncertainty, but they cannot be embarrassed.

In embarrassment, a person loses the relation to his situation, for the time being, and externally, but for the moment radically. No matter what particular motives are decisive, and no matter what effect his embarrassment may have on him (sometimes it's very funny), the interruption of contact, the experience of disconnection and disparity, is enough to evoke laughter. The person acknowledges a disorganization in relation to his "position," his "state of being," which, in view of the mediative role of his body, also affects the relation to the body. As the expression of laughter is itself a source of embarrassment to the laugher, it becomes an adequate reaction to—an embarrassment.

What we said above now finds its application: If the situation lacks clarity, if it becomes ambiguous in itself—and the "intersection" in embarrassment is a characteristic case of ambiguity—then language and gesture, action and expressive movement, break down. In such situations, lacking context, the reference in terms of which man must find a relation to his physical existence necessarily slips away. Disorganization is at hand.

That here laughter is only embarrassment is shown by the fact that a person who is embarrassed can just as easily burst into tears. To be sure, this will happen more readily with children and weak, naïve characters than with those of disciplined temperament who do not at once capitulate and feel sorry for themselves. With such people the consciouness of distance and "askewness" prevails, and this, in turn, results in a certain timidity and perplexity, to which smiling or laughing with a certain nuance are suited. These people are constantly exposed to embarrassment without—like the person who cries—succumbing to it or "leaving the field." That both kinds of expression are only reactions to embarrassment is clear, moreover, from the fact that they can be replaced by blushing, perspiring, and the like. Embarrassment has no exclusive reservoir of expression at its disposal. Otherwise, it would betray itself in its expression, and the expression would be untrue to it. Embarrassment in its expression must be—embarrassed; hence it can just as well laugh as cry, and still find the right expression in both cases.

Despair, on the other hand, is in no embarrassment about expression. Every expression suits it because none can suit it. Embarrassment still leaves the embarrassed person a certain latitude of expression, within which he ineptly presents himself. The situation is unanswerable but not threatening; there is no reason to lose one's head. But for the despairing person, who no longer knows where to turn, there is no latitude for expression. He can try anything and nothing, and perhaps silent despair is deeper. If he summons up energy to beat his breast, to rage, to cry or to laugh, he has not yet given himself up for lost, for he is still actualizing a distance from his situation. His brain reels, but he is not completely at the end of his rope. Admittedly weeping is here more "natural," because it indicates surrender and relief from tension, while the hard, hollow, tormented laughter of despair sounds unnatural and hellish, because it rings of defiance, mockery, or fraud. But in despair itself, which has found no outlet either in self-surrender or gallows humor, laughing and crying are equally relevant and equally out of place.

Unanswerable and threatening situations cause vertigo. We

capitulate before such situations as persons; we lose our heads. But it is only in despair that we reach that boundary which divides the zone of perplexity and hopelessness from true capitulation. Before we cross it, we fall into the impossible state of being completely trapped, a state in which no expression is any longer suitable. The disorganization of the relation between man and environment prevents an organized relation of the person to his body. Thus—just as in embarrassment, but with increased force—the expressive reactions of disorganization, laughing and crying, overcome the victim of despair. But the reactions are not to be confused with those of gallows humor or self-surrender. For in them we have conquered our despair—from above or below—and have perhaps attained that peace of ultimate renunciation which seals the reconciliation of opposites, the unity of victory and defeat, a reconciliation which we express by smiling amid our tears.

6. The Releasing Moment

With all due precautions against attempts to reduce the results of our individual analyses to summarizing formulae or, if we can, to define in a few words what at bottom really releases laughter and what is common to its different occasions, we can venture to say provisionally:

Only those boundary situations excite laughter which, without being threatening, are nevertheless unanswerable, so that the person is prevented from becoming their master and doing anything with them. Otherwise there are only two possibilities: *either* the situation is such that we can enter into it intellectually or emotionally, by examining or manipulating it, by means of words or actions, gestures or expressive movements; *or* we can no longer do this—the situation becomes intolerable and compels us to flee. In the first case, we can somehow cope with the situation; we can deal with it, successfully or unsuccessfully—at any rate, we accept it. In the second case, the situation overpowers us; we either flee from it, no matter how—we give up, lose our heads, turn giddy—or are destroyed by it.

Unanswerableness, coupled with the lack of an immediate threat to our existence, is the necessary, but not yet sufficient, condition which a situation must fulfill if it is to provoke laughter. *If the situation exercises no constraint* on a person, he will be able to stand aside from it with no expenditure of energy. The severance which shows itself in laughter—in laughter a person puts "paid" to the actual situation, i.e., acknowledges *and* breaks out of it—takes place against resistance. Only this resistance explains the tension which is released in laughter, and it is in turn related to the constraint which the situation exerts upon us. It holds us fast and at the same time forbids any possibility of our entering into it. Terms like ambivalence, ambiguity, equivocality, and confusion of meanings bear upon this antagonism between constraint and unanswerableness.

It is conceivable that this antagonism might be evoked by different properties of the situation, perhaps a strong excitation of phantasy in the absence, for example, of any logical context, or, again, a disclosure of important prospects of gain in the absence of all possibility of taking advantage of them. With such a distribution of constraining and repelling factors among dissociated characteristics or responsibilities, the existence of an insurmountable tension between man and his situation would always be a matter of accident or obstruction. This tension establishes a relation of frustrated seriousness but not out-and-out lack of seriousness. The latter corresponds only to the *internal* antagonism between constraint and repulsion. Unanswerableness and constraining power must not characterize a boundary situation only in this or that respect but must constitute its nature. The conditions which make a solution impossible in such a case also determine its constraining power. Only such situations provide occasions for laughter.

At its purest, the liberating effect of the intersection of their repelling and attracting character reveals itself in comic situations and in joking, where the antagonism between intuitive clarity and ambiguity of meaning is developed—the antagonism between sense and sense. Objectively, the intersection appears in a face, an action, a remark, or a train of thought. Even if we find ourselves, our position, our being and doing funny and humorous, we move inwardly away from ourselves and come to have an objective distance from ourselves. In funny and amusing situations, we are observers and hearers, in some cases of ourselves. Thus we can be involved (as objects) and yet be uninvolved, i.e., be only eyes and understanding (as subjects)—provided we have a sense of humor. To the extent that comedy and humor appeal to our apprehension, they create for it a special situation which both accommodates *and* conflicts with the conditions of apprehension in whatever is the appropriate way. The reason that laughter reveals itself here in its purest and freest form is doubtless to be found in that aesthetic distance which lays claim only to our contemplation and apprehension and even lets us sit in the orchestra while we ourselves stand on the stage.

In the consciousness of the noninvolvement of observer and listener (who is nevertheless involved!) we feel ourselves secure —a consciousness which ceases with humorless people as soon as it is a case of their own concern. The pleasure of having to do with something which is of no concern to us, of making merry at the expense of others—that cheapest and basest mode of sociability, which has, most unjustly, acquired a small halo from Bergson's interpretation of laughter as derision—and the pharisaism of feeling superior, of being able to rise above all and sundry through one's own sense for wit and humor: all of these adjuncts to the security of contemplation remove from laughter every inhibition. In play, on the other hand, or again in embarrassment, to say nothing of the situations of titillation or despair, the preoccupation and participation of the whole man prevails too strongly for him to be able to laugh from a full heart and without restraint. His laughter sounds forced, irritable, and distrait. He is not free enough to enjoy to the full the lightheartedness of the situation itself.

Thus the curve of laughter stretches from the mediate occasions of boundless joy and titillation to the boundary situations of embarrassment and despair. The top of the curve, which is correlated with the occasions of the comic and of wit and humor, indicates laughter in its full development. But that is no reason to view other kinds of laughter simply in the light of this type. Its emphatically cheerful character follows from the special detachment of the observer and listener which prepares the right ground for surrendering to the power of the expressive reaction.

Laughter as such is indeed pleasurable, but not cheerful, even if it usually acquires this affective tone. It is pleasurable as the release of a tension, which, in the superabundance of joy, springs from the drive to movement, in titillation from the ambivalence of sensuous excitation, in play from the intermediate state between freedom and constraint, in the case of the comic and the humorous from the ambiguous transparency of the appearance (and therefore from the appeal to our power of comprehension), and finally in embarrassment and despair from the intersection of the survey of a situation and helplessness to deal with it. Laughter is pleasurable and "healthy" as a reaction of letting oneself go in a physical automatism, as a surrender of the controlled unity of man and body, which demands a constant expenditure in inhibition and in drives. Finally, it is pleasurable as the answer, significant in its radical and uninhibited nature, in its very emancipation from the person, to a situation in the face of which every other answer fails.

For the rest, the evaluation of the various occasions of laughter must remain free from attempts to systematize. Our scale takes into account only the fact that laughter gains freedom and serenity, intensity and depth, with increasing distance of the individual from its occasion but loses these with decreasing distance, i.e., with growing fixity and fascination. Emotional participation can endanger the unequivocal nature of laughter. Intense joy or despair lead just as easily to weeping as to laughter. The same observation may be made with intense excitement as such. Despite other possibilities of expressive movement, rage, anger, and hypertension can be discharged in "nervous" laughter or weeping. The vital system of man is deeply disturbed by such states, its unity is disorganized "from below." Thus overfatigue works like overexertion or extreme excitement: the individual loses his composure and then (as in drunkenness) begins to laugh or cry—not because he feels merry or sad, but because he has lost control over his body. At the same time, of course, there is also the possibility of a change in consciousness and hence of laughter or tears motivated by it (therefore, not directly but only indirectly induced by the vital system).

If we equate—as we ought not to do—human distance from the occasion with coldness of feeling, then the often expressed opinion that laughter lacks warmth appears correct. But in fact it is not a matter of the quality and depth of feeling but of a strict association of laughter with consciousness, which in turn evokes the appearance of coldness. The occasions of titillation (in its various forms), of play, of comedy, and of wit and humor, even when they use unconscious *material,* remain, humanly speaking—that is, in relation to the center of the person, which he experiences only when something essential is at stake—on the periphery, the area of sense impression and sensation, of perception and fancy, of apprehension and thought. So even the most heartfelt, the most humorous laughter, which wells up out of the depths of feeling, retains a certain superficiality. Man answers directly with laughter, without implicating himself in the answer. In laughter he becomes anonymous, so to speak, a ground for the infectious energy dwelling within him.

Time and again, allusion has been made to the close connection of laughter with the understanding (Schopenhauer), to its instinctive tendency to the universal (Bergson). This tendency, it was said, should be explained now by the general character of the occasion, above all, of the comic occasion, and by the intellectuality in wit, now by the close relation of the laugher to society, since he requires others to laugh with him if he is to enjoy his laughter to the full. This may be confirmed within certain limits. The laughing person is open to the world. The consciousness of separation and isolation which frequently appears as a consciousness of superiority signifies at one and the same time detachment from the given situation and openness or flexibility. Disengaged in this way, man tries to engage others. And it is not a matter of chance that the outbreak of laughter begins immediately, more or less "apoplectically," and, as if to express the openness of the laugher, rings out into the world as he exhales. Crying, on the other hand, begins gradually, because it is mediated, and, as the expression of estrangement from the world and of isolation, develops in the movement of inhalation.

4 / Occasions of Crying

1. The Mediated Character of Crying

IN LAUGHTER, man puts "paid" to a situation. He answers it with laughter directly and impersonally. He falls into an anonymous automatism. He himself doesn't really laugh; there is laughter in him, and he is only theater and receptacle, as it were, for this occurrence. Crying is different. Here also man provides an answer by giving way to an anonymous automatism, which begins more or less slowly but can gain control of him. But now man includes himself in this answer. He participates within himself—he is moved, touched, shaken. When he chokes up and the tears come, he lets himself go inside; he is overcome and gives way to his tears.

This strange and unique relation to ourselves, for which we have very apt idioms like "capitulation," "giving up in defeat," "letting oneself go," "losing self-control," and so on, differentiates crying from laughing in its inner structure and in accord with the significance of the two reactions. Naturally this act of self-surrender is more easily induced in children, women, the old, the sick, and very emotional individuals than in self-controlled and reserved natures. But it remains, in every case, the deciding condition which gets crying started or makes it possible. It is a causative and a constitutive factor in one. Such an act is absent in laughter, which overcomes us directly and directly follows its occasion.

This fact should be kept in mind from the beginning. In the first place, it contains a warning against attempts to look for occasions of crying in the same way as those of laughter. Certainly there are such specific occasions, but, since they operate only mediately through a centrally oriented act of the human person, their demarcation and "characteristic" cannot be effected merely on the *objective* level (to which the occasions of laughter, except for joy and despair, belong). Secondly, the recognition that crying is mediated implies a difficulty for our thesis that, as a reaction to catastrophe, crying is akin to laughter and like laughter but, in contrast to it, presents a disorganization in the relation of man to his body. For if in crying man implicates himself in the answer because he no longer has himself in hand, lets himself go inwardly and thus automatically capitulates, still the disorganization, even if not avoided, seems to be released by an *encompassing act* of the person. In laughter, the dominant relation to the body is disrupted; in crying, on the other hand, man himself gives it up. But how can this self-surrender (half-voluntary, half-forced) lead to a disorganization if the person as a whole still stands behind it?

Nearly all who have seriously studied the phenomenon of crying—and in comparison with the number who have studied laughter they are surprisingly few—have been struck by its mediated character. They recognize that an act oriented to the person, a reflexive act, must be inserted between the occasion and the outbreak. We do not simply burst out crying but feel a weakness, a yielding coming on, which we either master or can no longer master. Laughter, too, can be suppressed, i.e., impeded in its full development. But still, even in its beginning stages, it is already there; it has already laid hold of us. For weeping to come to this, an internal loosening, detachment, and capitulation in the face of the overwhelming occasion must already have preceded; otherwise we would not feel ourselves growing weak. To try to degrade this difference between the immediacy of laughter and the mediacy of crying into a difference of degree, or to trace it back to the difference between their respective physical mechanisms of expression, is impossible. Precisely when we recognize in laughing a particular stress on the animal functions, above all on the muscular system, and in crying on the vegetative functions, above all on the secretory system, we must still have a sharp eye for the inner differences, which do not reflect the external but are independently coordinated with them.

Between occasion and outburst, a self-directed act of surrender must be inserted if I am to cry. How is this self-direction to be understood? Obviously, it not only triggers crying but is constitutive for it.

Up to now, two answers have been given to this question. One, uncomplicated and corresponding to the general view, was best formulated by Johann Edward Erdmann: [22] we laugh only at others; we weep only about ourselves. That is: at others because we find *them* funny and and laughable, ourselves naturally not; and about ourselves because we love ourselves best and experience only our own pain as pain. The other answer, more complicated, but nearer to the truth, comes from Schopenhauer: [23] weeping springs from a sympathy with oneself. My own pain does not directly make me weep but must first be projected as foreign, i.e., must become suffering, in order that I may project myself into it and then suddenly perceive it afresh as my own suffering. Such is the internal constitution of the "I feel sorry for myself" which evokes my tears. Led astray by the obvious but much too narrow notion that crying is the expression of pain and constitutes the antithesis of laughter as the expression of pleasure, both answers make the act of inner capitulation, of letting oneself go, an instance of crying *about* oneself.

Three mistakes are involved in this view. First, we do not cry only because of pain, sorrow, misery, and grief, but—if perhaps less often—because of joy, happiness, strong emotion, or extreme pleasure. Secondly, we do not laugh only at others because they are funny; in general, it is not only comic or humorous occasions that we laugh at. We laugh at ourselves too, if we have a sense of humor. This capacity for self-distance is precisely the touchstone of humor and its true source. Thirdly, the inner act of letting oneself go as the condition of crying (about whomsoever or whatsoever, on this or that occasion) is not to be confused with crying about oneself. The turning back to oneself which leads to loss of control, and feeling sorry for oneself, finding oneself pitiable, or, indeed, experiencing pain about oneself, are two different things.

The popular opinion starts from the premise that everyone is closest to himself and capitulates, loses his composure, in the last analysis, only in the shock of pain. Pleasure and its modifications lift the individual out of himself, make life easy for him, and allow him to forget himself. Pain and its modifications, on the other hand, throw him back upon himself, confine him within the limits of his physical and psychical existence, make his life burdensome to him, and constantly draw his attention to himself. Crying is nothing else but a transformation of the howling of the tormented creature in us, and thus, when all is said and done, is a crying about ourselves, i.e., about the physical or mental pain felt in ourselves—even though the occasion may be external, in the sight of another's sorrow, in the distress of our fellow man. Erdmann's account remains within this biological restriction of the sensation of pain.

Schopenhauer, on the other hand, tries to conceive the human character of crying by recognizing in it precisely a conquest of this animal constraint. By virtue of his imagination, his love, and his capacity for pity, the individual breaks through his proximity to himself and becomes so reconciled to his weakness, as it were, that he weeps at himself "as at another." That the individual can be reduced to tears only by his own affliction—this truth stands fast for Schopenhauer as well. Alien pain touches us only insofar as it becomes our own. Our power of sympathy does not go so far as to let us be moved to tears in direct perception of another's woes. "It hurts" must hold for us before we can feel sorry. But we differ from animals, in that we cannot only cry out in pain, not only scream and howl, but can also weep; not for pain, but for sorrow. The inner act of letting oneself go is in itself threefold. It transfers my own pain into the withdrawal of imaginative presentation and so turns it into suffering, alien suffering. It places me into sympathy with this alien suffering so that, through the power of sympathy, I assimilate to myself something that originally belonged to me. And finally, it communicates to me the perception that it is my own suffering which I sympathize with as alien.

In order to be able to shed tears about something, I must be sorry. In order to be able to be sorry, I must be sorry for myself. To this extent, Schopenhauer is a subjectivist. Man cries (and is thus distinguished from animals) because he feels compassion. In weeping, he does not think only about himself, or feel only himself; he is not absorbed only in himself, but feels beyond himself. To be moved himself, he lives in the other, and from others, and discovers in this return to himself, in this reunion with himself, his own pain as his own suffering. He weeps because he weeps for himself as sufferer. He does indeed stand outside his biological confinement by the limits of individual existence, but still he suffers only insofar as he suffers in and from himself.

A theory of weeping which does not from the start break through the horizon of pain and suffering runs the risk of being one-sided, no matter what its position vis-à-vis the special question of the relation of the perception of pain and suffering (with regard to oneself and others) to sympathy. What have the tears of love, worship, deep emotion, or joy in common with the tears of vexation, homesickness, melancholy, or indeed of physical pain? Certainly not the motivation of sorrow. The cause of crying must therefore be sought in another direction. To this end, an unbiased survey of the types of occasions and the varieties of crying and of the attempts to classify them is first necessary.

2. Attempts at Classification

The sequence of levels: body—soul [*Seele*]—mind [*Geist*] offers a natural guide to the attempts at classification. Between the purely physical occasions (of pain, shock, fatigue, and, in general, weakness following exertion or because of hunger, excitement, etc.) and the purely mental or intellectual ones (for example, deep emotion before a work of art, a person, or an event, or prayer and devotion) lies the sphere of affective occasions of crying which spring from the inner life of the person: his excitations, feelings, and emotional states. Without denying that all the levels act together in man's conscious existence and that every level can again become active on its own, we should not leave entirely out of account Charlotte Spitz's [24] idea that a developmental series of occasions for crying is laid down in this sequence of levels. The sequence then acquires the aspect of a developmental succession.

At the level of the genetically earliest reasons lies elemental crying, which is essentially determined by physiological conditions. Its end is as sudden as its onset is violent. Since it takes place at a certain remoteness from the ego, it accords with the structure of primitive, childish self-consciousness.

The next genetic level gives rise to personal crying, characteristic of a deepening of inward experience which begins with puberty. Emotions and feelings, moods and states, give self-consciousness greater independence of the external world but at the same time involve the person more intimately with it and make him more sensitive, more susceptible to its impressions and resistances.

As the last stage, we find the mentally or spiritually [*geistig*] determined weeping which results from deep emotion, prayer, or devotion and which presupposes a mature consciousness of self and world. The sense of value, of greatness, must be present as well as the ability to abstract from one's own interests. Here man first feels himself involved in his inmost being, yet no longer addressed as a personal I. The *thing itself* strikes him and moves him to tears—immediately, like the physical cause at the primitive level, but inwardly and without mediation by reactive feeling, without reference to the condition and situation of his own person.

Naturally, this allusion to the predominant claim of physical occasions in the first years of life, of psychical and emotional ones in the proper developmental period, and of spiritual occasions in the mature individual should not be understood as implying that the small child cannot weep out of fear or the grown-up because of toothache. Man is a whole at every stage of his development. It is only that in the very first years of life the physical state prevails; then—hidden under hundreds of masks—the inner life predominates, called forth by the cleavage between one's own development and the exacting, inhibiting adult world, through the awakening of sexuality; and finally, though differently in men and women, a being grounded in mental life, i.e., the sense of reality, of the good things of life and of "objective" values, the readiness for sacrifice. At age ten we no longer cry when we fall down, but we do cry from wounded pride. At thirty, provided we still have tears, we weep at the greatness of a line of poetry, the goodness of a person, from pity, remorse, and joy. And the more mature we become, the more ashamed we are—among men at least—of tears of physical or emotional suffering.

Possibly this is connected with the authority of the masculine point of view in highly developed cultures. Women may weep more easily for personal reasons and preserve this ability significantly longer than men do. And whether it is borne or welcomed, but in any case respected, their reputation as the weaker sex with strongly developed feelings has been firmly established in popular psychology. Woman (who matures earlier than man, but seldom gets as far as he) has a comparatively childlike, elemental nature, that stays close to life. Hence in male-dominated cultures she is always allowed to count irrationality among her privileges. Emotionality and strong feeling the masculine world concedes to the female, at any rate to the extent to which she denies it to herself—leaving open here the question of what is reality and what ideology.

Personal crying develops in its profusion of forms at this level of feelings, moods, and passions, and it is no accident that neither physically nor mentally induced crying (in the immediacy already mentioned) can rival the wealth of forms characteristic of personal crying. Charlotte Spitz proceeds from Rudert's differentiation of feelings according to the type of their dynamics and separates the more relaxed, fluid, and freely oscillating feelings from those which are more tense, choked up, or sluggish and easily exhaustible—though of course intersections and interfusions are also possible between them. She distinguishes four groups as principal forms: tense, predominantly tense, predominantly relaxed, and relaxed crying, following Wundt's principle of the polarity of tension and relaxation. The degree of tension involved in crying she considers as determined by the basic emotions or feelings.

The first of the four types of crying, that characterized by tension, is marked by a very agitated frame of mind with pronounced clarity of consciousness. For the most part, this type is forcibly aroused against the background of an unyielding, choked-up tension or a paralytic rigidity and takes place as a violent outburst. If an accommodation occurs, then the person involved matures inwardly. In the absence of such an accommodation, bitterness and exhaustion remain. Two subtypes may be distinguished, of which the first reveals a more distressful, choked-up crying, the second a more sluggish, exhaustible variety. The first subtype accords with sthenic-activating occasions like pain, rage, and hate, the second subtype with asthenic-paralyzing occasions like impotence, apathy, hopelessness, and perplexity. Anxiety and despair can have now an activating, now a paralyzing, effect.

As a fundamental characteristic of the second type of crying, that marked by a predominance of tension, the person involved likewise has a complete comprehension of his internal state and clarity of consciousness. But the internal freedom to look at oneself is repressed by the necessity of coming to terms with occurrences which do not arise from the internal state alone. Pain, remorse, worry, grief, vexation, disappointment, and sometimes compassion are here the characteristic occasions either of a crying which begins suddenly—if in a flash a person become aware of his changed position—or of a crying predisposed by emotion, which arises slowly for comfort and consolation. The tears are bitter and do not free a person from a sense of aggrievement, do not eliminate "the ache in one's heart."

Mourning, sadness, melancholy, and self-pity lead to the third type of crying, the predominantly relaxed. Here, in place of clarity of consciousness, there prevails, along with a decrease in tension of the internal state, a comprehension open to interpretation. The person involved is affected by mood, and he experiences this affection or "attunement" by a more intimate involvement with external events. At the high point of this emotional excitement, he is overcome by tears, in which he finds reassurance, absorption, and peaceful resignation. In contrast to the attitude of mind characteristic of the second type of crying, feelings here have no real depth (also no narrowness). Instead of enduring emotions, impulsive feelings predominate; a person feels warm at heart.

The fourth type of crying is the relaxed, which arises from longing, sadness, melancholy, and the need for consolation. With this type, one submits willingly to his tears. At one time they may well up out of the depths of sincere feeling as tears of joy, at another out of a lesser depth as feelings of alleviation and reconciliation. In its internal makeup this type of weeping is comparatively homogeneous, open, and unspecialized. In giving way to tears here, we are governed by a feeling of elevation and bliss.

In all four types of affective crying as they are said to develop at the middle or so-called personal level, the deficient and depressing, the dark, burdensome, and low-spirited modes of feeling predominate. What in conformity with the theory of suffering or sorrow is erroneously affirmed for all levels of crying, whether physically, subjectively, or personally determined, seems therefore to hold at least for this middle level of emotionally conditioned weeping—although with certain limitations. In point of fact, even here the limitations relative to exceptions like joy, love, surrender, devotion, rapture, and complex "spiritual feelings" like remorse or shame, are so significant that this law cannot be allowed to stand unquestioned. That man is reduced to tears cannot lie in a deficiency alone.

Only more deeply penetrating analyses of particular occasions of crying such as sympathy, grief, or remorse can break the spell of the "theory of suffering." The work of Balduin V.

Schwarz[25] shows how advantageous such a procedure is in seeking clarification of the structure of a "feeling" and how indispensable for an understanding of its power to induce weeping. This work too takes the concept of a graduated series from the physical through the subjective to the personal level as a guide for answering the question of what role the physiological component plays in the different types of weeping.

As long as the mechanism of peripheral release, i.e., of reflex-produced tears, has not been broken through, as, for example, in the squalling of small children, we cannot speak of true crying. On the other hand, the first type of crying, crying at physical pain, exhibits the effect of an unpleasurable feeling-tone. We feel ourselves delivered up to, shackled to, the body, not simply as a physical condition but also as a theme, not as a "nervous" disturbance like overexertion or fatigue but as something about which we cry, or, as idiom has it even more subtly: for and because of which we cry. We cry for pain and because of pain.

The next type of crying has purely psychical causes, though the crying takes place, not simultaneously with the actual psychic events, but following them as an independent act. Here we find the weeping that follows anxiety, general exhaustion, terror. "My nerves are still quivering!" The welling-up of tears produces an easing of tension which has the effect of a response without being given as one. For here, as in the first type of crying, the physical event fails to be wholly permeated by the mental act.

Only the third type reveals crying in its fully developed form. Here it stands in immediate association with the psychical act. Expression and vital discharge affect each other and pass over into each other. It is in this way that affective crying is constituted, i.e., the type which, in Spitz's schema, already belongs to the middle level of personal weeping. Among all occasions of affective weeping, it is grief which occupies the lowest place on the scale, since in weeping for grief the physiological still predominates. Its expression is grounded in more contingent elements (such as inner excitation and emotional surrender before the superior power of misfortune) but not in the really essential elements of the psychical attitude of grief itself. In this general area belong other related forms of mental pain and sad yearning.

The emotions of fury, rage, defiance, and despair may give rise to impotent weeping, which in the case of rage and fury replaces the normal abreaction in vital discharge (if not through a specific expression, still in the form of the discharge of tension). It guides the reaction opposed to the normal "sthenic" attitude of these emotions. Decisive for defiance and despair, along with a rigid, distorted posture, is an impotent agitation which is discharged in convulsive weeping. Tears of mortification also reveal a similar expressive saturation of the physical process. A man is hurt on some point of central importance to him. Corresponding to this, as it were, pointed wound, his crying shows a constricted, cramped character, as if under a pressure that will not give way.

From this point on, the automatism characteristic of the physiological in the schema of crying recedes, and the element of expression comes to the fore. Tears no longer flow because we see ourselves shackled and oppressed, imprisoned within the confines of our body or of an oppressive situation, hemmed in by obstacles, and affected by reactions, but because we have been granted deliverance. In this way, the weeping of peripeteia comes into being as a fourth type. The human being steps forth —specifically, in acts which take place "in a moment"—out of a fundamental stance. Either he actively brings about an inner conversion, which is clearly distinct from any mere shift in mood, or he passes from a tense to a relaxed posture, from harshness to gentleness, from despair to hope. The classic example of peripeteia is remorse.

The initial act of conversion relaxes the psychic tension and changes its meaning for the person who relaxes in it. The act of weeping need no longer take place simultaneously with this inner revolution, but is the adequate expression (which in consequence can even be absent!) of it. There is also the possibility that the liberating effect may be triggered by an objective force. A case in point is crying for joy (e.g., of lovers reunited, of the prisoner released, of the joyful emotion of a great moment).

If the fourth type of crying lacks the emotional tone and excitement of the third, nevertheless it still decidedly preserves a specific reference to the individual person. It is I in whom the sudden change takes place, who makes the conversion. The crying characteristic of deep emotion, compassion, love, devotion, and worship goes far beyond this. The weeping of the fifth type, which corresponds approximately to the personally determined weeping of Spitz's schema, lacks any properties that can be related to the discharge of tension in the emotions. The vehemence and abruptness of expression disappears. Henceforth it is a matter of evaluative responses which concern simply the qualities of what is found moving, touching, lovable, or holy, without reference to thee and me. To be sure, the truth of the values in question is not decisive for the authenticity of the expression, but only the veracity and sincerity of the relation to values to which one has found one's way. Consequently, as far as value-qualities go, genuine deception as to value also reveals itself in the expression, as we can see, for example, in sentimental lachrymosity, which is different from genuine (objective) compassion.

The Schwarzian scale ends with the fifth type—a scale of the psychical incorporation and refinement of the physical expressive process of weeping. We have attained an adequate survey of the essential occasions of crying. And without seeing in this survey anything more than an attempt at classification which offers satisfactory points of departure, we can take off from it in our analysis of the releasing factors. At least its scrupulousness should assure us breadth of vision.

3. The Resonance of Feeling

We must remember at this point that the entire investigation of the occasions of crying stands under the limiting condition that these occasions are not in themselves sufficient to induce crying but require the individual's own act of inner capitulation. Thus pain, sorrow, grief, yearning, despair, vexation, remorse, overwhelming emotion, love, and worship do indeed include moments which are preconditions for the onset of crying but still are not sufficient. Although such preconditions are grounded in the essential nature of these feelings and affections—for it is not a question here merely of favorable dispositions for the release of tears but of specific occasions which brook no response but precisely this—it is not necessary that any one of them join with, or issue in, crying. Pain and joy, love and despair, can, in their full authenticity and power, take possession of a man without moving him to tears.

Schwarz expressed this insight as follows: "The constituents of weeping, therefore, must be in determinate moments which qualify the concrete performance of an act in a contingent way, specifically, so that these moments are able to take effect only in this determinate series of acts on the basis of their nature." The decisive factors or conditions definitive for crying (its constituents) do not lie in the pain or joy, etc., themselves but in something additional which alters the pain or joy "in an external way," whereby it is to be noticed that this additional something cannot be joined to everything psychical, without respect to its content, but only to the affections and feelings mentioned, precisely on the basis of their particular nature.

In this addendum—which is not just casual or now and then—lies the "substance" of crying. We have acknowledged it so far as the act of internal letting-go and surrender, carried out by the person involved, an act based on aspects taken partly from the object, partly from the subject. From wherever an affect or feeling of the group in question (to which, for example, envy or enthusiasm do not belong) results in crying, this results from a kind of captivation by the facts in which the "normal" distance to objects has broken down. They press in on me; I give myself up to them. This mode of distanceless captivation by things is not to be confused with the intensity of a sensation or a passion. A strong, hyperdistinct, painfully significant impression is, for example, still far from being a shattering, gripping, moving, and poignant impression.

Schwarz distinguishes two modes of being touched: the mode of incision [*Einschneiden*] (as it is present, perhaps, in physical pain or hurt feelings) and the mode of free letting-oneself-be-touched, as in being moved, gripped, convulsed, and overpowered by emotion. In both modes, the typical emotional or affective link with objects develops, in which subject and object no longer oppose each other, but man and world interpenetrate—in which it is not the "understanding" but the "heart" that speaks. In both modes of being touched, man is delivered up to a force against which he must "keep himself in hand," must maintain his upright posture, if it is not to overpower him.

Since this inner capitulation is grounded in the nature of the emotions and feelings, or joined to them, there is a whole scale of modifications which encompasses the inner habitus of the process of "being reduced to tears." Thus, for grief and mental anguish, Schwarz finds an "overflow," for rage and fury, a "being shaken and then giving up in defeat," for despair, "confusion," although the persons involved in all these cases experience no inner transformation in other respects. Only in the tears of peripeteia does one really capitulate in the face of an appropriating power. In joy, for example, we are overwhelmed and experience the expansive-explosive force of liberation.

Is it because of the dominant power of an emotion that we

haul down our colors before it, or does the emotion only play the role of transmitting a reality, an objectivity and value property, so that while we indeed weep from pain or joy, and so on, we still weep *at* something? Up to this point, it might appear that the feeling and the act of capitulation were in themselves sufficient to produce our tears. They are indeed sufficient; only we should not overlook the fact that the feeling has as its foundation, as Schwarz terms it, a distanceless captivation by things.

Feeling is essentially binding myself to something, a binding which allows me far less independence of things, people, values, thoughts, or events than does visualization, perception, or any otherwise motivated attitude to objects. Feelings like sorrow, joy, indignation, enthusiasm, contempt, admiration, rage, compassion, hate, or love are precisely (and this as opposed to Schwarz) not "attitudes" of a person to objects on the basis of particular qualities which strike him but resonant appeals [*durchstimmende Angesprochenheiten*] to which the person is more or less exposed according to his individual temperament and which he can resist, if occasion arises, only by main strength.

As resonant appeals the emotions (feelings or affects in the broader sense) can vary according to intensity and degree of excitement. Beyond this, they can be genuine or false. False feelings have nothing to do with myself. Yet these false feelings give rise to tears more easily than the genuine. Sentimentality, which is out to be touched and misses no opportunity to enjoy inner capitulation, scarcely permits true feelings to arise. For true feeling is an appeal bound through and through to what is the case. Not the resonance alone, with its qualities of mood, like cheerful, gloomy, joyful, irritated, sad, etc., governs our state, but the resonant appeal of some particular quality. In false feeling there is no appeal in an objective context, and only the resonance itself absorbs us.

Genuine emotions are bound to situations or objects (though naturally not objectively on the basis of doubt and decision) and are central. They have to do with myself; I am absorbed in them and appealed to by them. This centrality allows (in the first place) scope for fluctuations in intensity. My love can be deeply rooted, and then it is strong; it can be fleeting and superficial, and then it is weak. In both degrees of strength, however, I participate, and as a whole man. This participation, this pledging of myself, this centrality, is lacking only if the feeling is false (and even a superficial, weak feeling can be genuine).

In the second place, centrality as a formal constituent of genuine feeling allows scope for variations in degree of excitement. There is quiet anger, quiet love, and so on, plus the corresponding more tempestuous forms. The latter are called affects in the narrower sense. Impetuosity and abruptness with a manifestly strong connection with vital expressions (blushing, turning pale, sweating, palpitations, panting, play of facial muscles, gesticulation, and, not least, the flow of tears) give these affects their characteristic stamp. But the more passionate feelings are not on this account more genuine or deeper than the less passionate.

Not only are feelings not motivated attitudes; they are not attitudes at all, but resonant appeals to man as a whole. Although a feeling may be unjustified and unjust, it is never without content.[26] The content is formed by some quality that addresses the person, that is, speaks to him, a quality which he does not at once reject and to which he reacts appropriately. If it is only his own body that is sensuously involved, whether pleasurably or painfully, a person is not addressed or appealed to but merely engrossed or affected. We can be appealed to by something—we usually use this term, to be sure, to denote a comfortably agreeable quality, in the sense of "being taken with something," but here it is employed in a wider and formal sense—when we encounter an objective quality. There are no limits of content here. A landscape, a melody, a face, a piece of news, a thought, can direct this "invitation" to me just as well as my own state, the immediately tasted pleasure in which I delight, the experienced pain under which I find myself suffering.

Distanceless captivation by objects or objective events by means of feeling can consequently be cultivated only by a being that has a sense of objectivity. Although feeling is subjective, i.e., not bound to the standards of theoretical or practical attitudes, its subjectivity requires a distance to an objective sphere so that, in passing over it, it may link itself to the immediately available qualities of that sphere. Only where there is understanding can there also be heart. Animals feel pleasure and pain; they are often closely bound to familiar persons and circumstances and to that extent are affectionate. But they do not feel loyalty, friendship or enmity, jealousy, love or hate. Feeling as such is essentially human.

As a resonant appeal, feeling stands—and here we must differ with many theoreticians, including Schwarz, for example—

between "reaction" and "rejoinder." It is too loosely connected to the occasion to be a reaction which is triggered directly, like a reflex. It is not simply induced (by a stimulus) and set in motion, as it were; rather, a quality "speaks" to the person and awakens a resonance in him. And, again, the feeling is too intimately connected to the occasion to be a rejoinder. The occasion does not first evoke a personal attitude, and it creates no problematic situation, but causes the person (though from a distance, like an echo) to resound. As a commensurate oscillation in which the whole man is involved, more deeply or superficially, more calmly or with greater agitation, feeling occupies the mean between reaction and rejoinder, the two types of response known to life.

Rejoinder and reaction are related to each other as attitudinal and nonattitudinal behavior. Admittedly, quick-witted reaction to sudden danger, or to opportunities which suddenly present themselves, is certainly to be differentiated from reflex reactions in individual organs or limbs. If, for the latter, nature has devised automatic mechanisms which, by means of separate nerve circuits, cut off coordination between stimulus and reaction, then quick-wittedness requires the presence of the whole organism. Unconscious and conscious behavior, i.e., reflexive-partial and immediate-total response, are alike possibilities of active, significant conduct which is directed to the external world and need not be mediated by an "attitude." [27] Thus, both forms are to be found in the animal world. The old schema, which would restrict the conscious state to man and concede to animals only unconsciousness, i.e., the automatism of reflexes, is mistaken and has its origin in an overnarrow conception of consciousness. To be sure, only man shows conscious behavior in the sense of motivated conduct, channeled through attitudes. To the demands and questions raised by the environment, only he discovers the appropriate (objectively relevant) rejoinder.

The philosophers' difficulty in fitting feeling into the schema of consciousness-unconsciousness is symptomatic of the remarkable penetration by immediacy and inwardness, by distanceless captivation by things and by their appeal to us, which gives feeling its specific nature. Naturally, there are feelings that are not yet or no longer conscious, sprouting or suppressed, which—like convictions too, for instance—represent a certain psychic reality, constitute sources of strength or danger with which we have to reckon, whether we know it or not. But developed feeling does not of itself constitute a content of consciousness, nor is it excluded from it. We know "of it," or we don't know of it—the captivation of our selves through feeling is neither increased nor diminished. Reflection and analysis can mislead us in our feelings and finally undermine them, as a heightening of self-consciousness is certainly detrimental to the development of the life of feeling. Understanding and heart live at war with each other, and only in rare cases is an important decision possible without our facing the question of which voice we are to follow.

If we decide according to the norms of the understanding on the basis of a conscious attitude, then we are following the perspectives of consciousness. We reduce ourselves to the I of observation, of thought, planning, and inference, and reckon our own person as an object into the calculation. Feeling resists this formalization; in feeling, the whole man, deeply stirred by something and thoroughly attuned to it, appeals to a state of affairs, even before the I in him has found time to force upon him the distance of cool reflection. But the resistance of feeling has found no sanction before the tribunal of philosophy. In the long run, the various forms of irrationalism have not been able to prevail. For a conception of knowledge whose ideal is universal validity and demonstrability, just as for a conception of conduct which strives for universal obligation and lawfulness, feelings remain "subjective," limited to the inner aspect of the individual and of subordinate value as sources of knowledge. Only as the domain of art, and in certain theories of religion as medium of the personal certainty of faith, does feeling play a role in the rationalist tradition—to the detriment of the facts.

For there is no question that if psychology had not developed, under the dominance of the natural sciences, as a kind of natural science of the inner sense, it would have been spared the fixation of all its themes within the framework of consciousness, a framework oriented primarily to epistemology and cognitive psychology, and the psychology of feeling would have been less badly off. And had philosophy not so long regarded itself under the same ideals as psychology, i.e., as the epistemology of natural science, or had its reflections on man and the world not been conceived in constant reference to mathematics and physics, then the problematic of the whole man as a psychophysical unity would not have been so neglected in favor of a dualistic schema.

4. The Releasing Moment

Not all feelings can make us cry (as is shown by envy, hate, disdain, and contentment, for example) but only those in which we become aware of a superior force against which we can do nothing. This awareness of our own impotence must take the form of feeling; it must take hold of us and grip us in order to trigger the act of inner surrender which causes us to weep. Feelings move us to tears as ways of taking cognizance of and of being addressed by a threatening power, not as mere moods and inner agitations. Thus the superior force lies, neither in the intensity nor in the centrality nor yet in the degree of excitation of the feeling, but in the "objective quality" to which it immediately binds us.

In the state of physical pain, the force of its incisiveness and the helplessness of our exposure to it is evident. To be in pain is to be thrown back defenselessly on one's own body, and in such a way that one finds no further relation to it. The painful region seems excessively extended, it seems to overspread and entirely displace the remaining regions. We seem to consist of nothing but teeth, forehead, or stomach. Burning, boring, cutting, sticking, knocking, pulling, gnawing, vibrating, pain acts as an invasion, destruction, disorientation, a power swirling into a bottomless deep. Here, naturally, the inner capitulation can result either directly from our own disturbance, as in other cases of vital loss of equilibrium (exhaustion, overstimulation) or mediately through the perception of our own suffering. But even then we are not "hurting ourselves," nor do we feel sorry for ourselves. The matter stands too close to us for that.

Similar relations prevail with mental pain, above all in irreparable loss and insult. "One doesn't get over these things," "they rankle and gnaw at one," "they leave their sting behind"—and so on with all the idioms borrowed from the physical sphere. Here, in the consciousness of one's situation created by injury or loss, as by loneliness, impoverishment, humiliation, or injustice, feeling has space to develop fully. In situations of leave-taking and separation, the feeling of the pain of parting and of loneliness is changed to misery (homesickness, wistful yearning). Pain and misery bring grief in their wake when awareness of the overpowering force of the situation loses some of its burning intensity. Here, again, a person can be brought to the point of capitulation by being deeply moved, by loneliness and the like, directly or through becoming conscious of his own suffering.

Our own helplessness before an external force is still more graphically revealed in the emotional ferment of rage, fury, defiance, and despair. Here the rending, painful habitus of our own stiffness and aggression is suppressed, and in submitting we perceive in the ineffectiveness of the exhausted passion the hopeless and irrevocable nature of the circumstances. Often it is only the bodily feeling of exhaustion and debility that forces tears to one's eyes, but the feeling of futility is already sufficient —especially if it penetrates the rising emotion and reveals the hopelessness of resistance on our part.

In peripeteia, on the other hand, where the change is from attitudes of tension to relaxation (in remorse, unexpected joy, conversion), and when we are stirred by compassion, love, submission, and prayer, our own helplessness is harder to discover. For what we perceive in them is precisely the fact that nothing threatening and hostile now confronts us, to awaken our resistance. The world no longer exerts pressure on us. This, in the feeling that a burden is lifted and pressures slackened, in the feeling of overwhelming exaltation, our growing strength, the increasing scope of our own freedom, should really determine our human attitude and lend it support. But, in spite of this, we capitulate; we are able to capitulate. Before what?

This question is easiest to answer for the modes of overwhelming emotion, of submission and self-surrender. Before the sublimity of a work of art or a landscape, before the quiet power of the powerless simplicity of their being, before the fragile beauty, the touching candor and familiarity of children, we sink inwardly to our knees as before a grandeur that transcends every relation to ourselves. The encounter with them does not place us in situations we can do nothing with (like those that make us laugh, that cut the ground from under our feet by confusing the possibilities of action); they place us in situations where even the attempt to "do something" no longer arises.

The gripping, the touching, the loved, the high and holy are encountered as the absolutely unequivocal and yet distant, as the pure *end* for our usual behavior, attuned to proportionalities, relations, and relativities, to pressures and counterpressures. "Helplessness" before this is perhaps an unhappy word, since it makes it appear as if it were only a question of an inability to resist a force. And yet when tears come, we speak here too quite rightly of becoming soft and weak. In the disruption of the normal interrelatedness of our life in and with the world, which usually conceals from us the purity of the being of beings and the goodness of good things, we have arrived at a boundary of all behavior. If this disruption is not formed by some power within the world which pains and hurts us, but by powerlessness in essence, by rapture, by defenselessness, by rapprochement and the gift of grace, then we nevertheless encounter in it an ultimate boundary, an unconditioned end.

Essential for the onset of tears on such occasions is the sudden transition from an attitude of tension to one of relaxation. If in the course of life we have had to reckon with hostility and misfortune, disappointment and infamy, and have nevertheless not abandoned the fight for our own cause and our own happiness, we will feel the sudden easing of the world's accustomed pressure before images and works of nature and of art, before children, in church, and in love as doubly moving and overpowering. Thus men give way to such tears more readily than women because they spring from an unearned peace in the battle with the world.

At first sight, the same thing seems to hold for peripeteia. The inflexible attitude of stubbornness or recklessness which allows one to be carried away, the prolonged pressure of privation and joylessness, veer suddenly into a state of release. This sudden transformation shames us in our offensive or defensive attitude, now left without an object, and, in the contrast of our new with our old condition, is often associated with self-pity. With the deeply felt release of remorse and joy or of the rebirth of conversion, we become aware as well of joylessness endured, injustice committed, possibilities lost, life left unlived. Here the happiness of release and the weakness of submission are tinged with pain: pain for the irretrievable, which puts us at a distance from ourselves. This situation gives rise to what Schopenhauer mistakenly described as the universal reason for crying: the objectivation of one's own pain to a quasi-extrinsic suffering, to which I empathize, with which I sympathize, and in which I discover that it is myself I pity.

Thus what is decisive for the weeping of inner reversal is not only the relaxation of a tension, the loosening of an inflexibility, but the awareness of an irretrievable, ineffaceable, irrecoverable life. Without this awareness, in a knowledge akin to feeling, there would be no slackening of tension. Thus remorse is not simply pieced together from the knowledge: "I oughtn't to have done it, if only I hadn't done it," and the burning feeling of a futile wish to be allowed to start over; it is the original impact of being back at our starting point, at the radical position of beginning afresh, which we now try to clarify retroactively, but only in the schema of emotional and cognitive components. And what is true of remorse is also true of shame, of the overpowering joy of deliverance or reunion, of conversion. Their releasing effect arises from the contrast to the pressure which has slackened, the night which has been vanquished, and not only from the positive qualities of the new state into which we have been transposed. These feelings place us between two finalities in the irreversible stream of time. In the irrevocability of life we encounter our own finitude.

Finitude as incapacity, as helplessness, on this account speaks to us all the more forcefully, the closer it seems to be linked with the basic conditions of our existence. The child cries because he does not get something he wants, because he must do what he is told, because he is hurt or left alone. He experiences his own finitude only in the superior strength of external intervention. Only in the more mature individual does the insight first arise that his own primal being, the source of all his power and real (or presumptive) freedom, as well as his own initiative and his ability to reach out beyond himself, is at the same time his boundary, on which he founders. The tragic conflict, not simply between good and evil, freedom and world, as between external powers to which man is delivered, but between what he himself must be and do, on the one hand, and, on the other, what springs from this demand as destroying fate, as necessity through freedom: tragic conflict in this sense is thus an inexhaustible source of weeping, but weeping no longer directed to one's own person. Perhaps the Aristotelian analysis of the cathartic effect of pity and fear is too closely tied to temporal considerations. Perhaps pity and fear are already indications of an emotional state which lies deeper and is not occasioned by the fear of fate or pity for the hero in his downfall but, conversely, first evokes these emotions. However that may be, the encounter with the inevitable, which arises from man's risking of himself, is the moving element in the tragic conflict.

In the aesthetics of the tragic, the question has often been discussed, why the phenomenon of a necessity through freedom does not have a comic effect. Observed from a purely formal point of view, tragic and comic conflicts are closely related. Do the results of the conflict decide about its actual character, so that if they turn out favorably there is relieved laughter, whereas, if they turn out unfavorably, weeping is appropriate? Those who see more deeply into the matter have always disputed this answer. There are frightful catastrophes which appear extremely funny, even though the pity we feel would gladly stifle our swelling laughter. Take the case of the intrepid aeronautical engineer who, before a thousand attentive spectators, climbs into his machine in the closed hangar, gives the signal for the start, and in the next moment strikes the opposite wall. Following this tragic event is the thunderous laughter of amazement as the last salvo over the grave of the hero whose life has come to such an untimely end. Here, death enters, not as the end of a conflict, but as the ridiculous outcome of a provocation, caricatured as well by its mechanical effect. No genuine necessity through freedom governs here, but the power of the disproportion between an effort of the loftiest nature and the actual situation.

Freedom and necessity, undertaking and aptitude, beginning and end must be suitable to each other and take place on the same level of being. Only in this way is the level of seriousness maintained and all diversion to the superficial and the accidental avoided, diversions opposed to the iron necessity of fate. Despite this, physical nature, the unexpectedness of external circumstances to which we are exposed by body and soul, can still produce a tragic effect in comic conflict: witness the tragicomic. To those who have seen Chaliapin's film about Don Quixote, the ending remains unforgettable: the hero in his attack on the windmill transfixes himself with his lance on the sail, calling to mind as if by chance the image of one broken on the wheel, crucified by his own idea of knighthood, crucified by his own order and without redemption.

In tragic conflict—to the degree to which fate or its poet relinquishes villains, collisions with popular morality, and an oversimple world order—finitude is revealed as the basic condition of our existence. But it can also be revealed without conflict in all the ways in which we become emotionally aware of the transitoriness of life. To be sure, to our contemporaries, *Weltschmerz* belongs to a bygone age. They tolerate no feelings with universal pretensions, just as they find every expression of feeling embarrassing. And yet the feeling of the gone-by, the never-again, is alien to no one, even if it does not rise to the level of romantic nostalgia. Not even the most level-headed person is spared sadness and longing over departed youth.

It makes little sense to argue whether this feeling or the tragic approach to the power of fate makes possible a purer and more objective encounter with finitude. The resonant, direct appeal of finality and inevitability is common to both. Through both, the individual person feels himself lifted beyond his isolated and accidental existence and, in the certainty of his passing, at once humbled and exalted. Periods in which death lies in the streets and great upheavals and bitter hardship make plausible to men the worthlessness of existence sustain neither *Weltschmerz* nor tragedy. In such periods, they shun the tears which arise before the image of life, for they experience tears enough in its burdens and frustrations.

Tears are not always commensurate with a catharsis or with a resolution. The feeling of helplessness can be forthcoming at the end of a fruitless struggle or through a painful emotional impact. In peripeteia and encounters with the inimitable and the ultimate, it can be the expression of a blissful self-surrender before the overwhelming. Suffering (or, indeed, sympathy) is thus not a necessary condition, even if in most cases men sink under their finitude as under a burden and experience it as being hemmed in by barriers in pain, suffering, melancholy, and grief. What alone is decisive is the fact of being overpowered as a total emotional state to which man is delivered up without reserve, so that he is no longer able to stand at a distance and answer. But to lose one's composure in this case means to lose one's relation to the world, and one's self-control, in such a way that the loss is still visible in the expression.

5 / The Source of Laughing and Crying

1. Two Limits of Behavior

With the determination of the expressive character of laughing and crying and the motives which release them, our analysis has carried out at least the indispensable preparations for recognizing their source. Perhaps it has already uncovered that source and lacks only the proper perspective toward it or the right background against which it can be brought into relief as the source. Such analyses sharpen one's eyes, but they also narrow the visual field and deprive the observer of the proper overview, so that he finally loses the feeling for "where" he really is. For this reason, it is wise to recall once again the most important stages along the path to the depths, or the middle, of the subject, so that we can see what has been achieved and what is missing.

Laughing and crying form a unique genus of expression. As distinct from mimic movements, they represent utterances in which the loss of self-control reaches a particular level and attains a particular significance. Through this loss of control and lapse into a physical process which compulsively runs its course and is opaque in itself (in contrast to expressive movement, which is perhaps immoderate and uncontrolled but always symbolic), the relation of man to his body becomes disorganized. Yet this disorganized condition in which we are overcome and shaken up is not merely endured, but, like a gesture or meaningful reaction, is understood. We laugh and cry only in situations for which there is no other answer. That is, to the person who takes a word, an image, or a situation in such a way that he must laugh or cry, there is no other answer, even if others do not understand his mood, take him to be silly or sentimental, and find other types of behavior more to the point. For the person who laughs or cries, the actual situation is dominated by the effective impossibility of giving it any other suitable answer. Perhaps he could remain solemn and unmoved, only he does not choose to, and deliberately gives way to the comic or the affecting. But this is not crucial. What is really of importance is that statements, people, things, or events stimulate him to laugh or cry insofar as he can, or will, "do nothing more with them," yet nevertheless gives expression to this impossibility—an expression suited to this "being done with."

"Being done with," "being able to do nothing more with," does not imply, in this case, that one is at the end of one's patience, or of one's strength, or has had enough of a thing or a person; it means arriving at a boundary which thwarts every possibility of accommodation, not only in fact but on principle. Naturally, we can obtain an idea of the range of possibility of such accommodation and of the kind of limit involved only if we picture to ourselves the normal situation of human existence.

a) We consider a mode of existence normal in which we can orient ourselves, in the literal or figurative sense of the word. It must be familiar to us or be able to become so, and it must offer us scope enough so that we can do something with and in it. "World" as the stage on which human existence is played is traversed by a hazy boundary which separates the region of the familiar from the strange. In both regions, things need not always "go right"; and the familiar can become strange, and conversely. But there must be a play of relations between both spheres. We want to be certain that things are in some *condition* or other, even if we do not know (and perhaps never can know) exactly what. It may be that man has an inherent disposition to presume that everything has a purpose. But he will not always wish to determine this condition so narrowly. For nature, and human concerns as well, not only makes mock of our notions of what is purposeful, but also, in many areas, of purposefulness as such. And it would also be unwarranted to consider this world logical within the limits of conceptual exactitude and corrigibility. But what man, even as a being who names, and certainly as a being caring and cared for, planning and asking, cannot dispense with is that all that befalls, surrounds, and sustains him should be in *some* condition. The opposite would be pure chaos —perhaps the proper outlook and delight of gods and philosophers, but certainly not the medium of his life.

That things are in a certain condition implies that we are able to rely on them because they are this and not that, and that we are able to do something with them. It means that we can address something as something—at the risk that it may disclaim the address; or make something into something—at the risk that it may elude our grasp; or let something pass current as something—at the risk that it may turn out to be something else. Life reckons with this capacity for organization, this stability and flexibility, with a minimum of definitiveness and elasticity, order and pliability, closure and openness. The medium in which it is to develop can be neither absolutely unyielding and complete, nor absolutely fluid and indeterminate. It must offer stopping points, footholds, taking-off places, pauses, safeguards—also to escape from and to oppose. If we want to call this a minimal requirement of rationality (with which the world luckily complies), we may do so. But in order not to fall into the error of equating rationality with a certain kind of intellectual or functional logic, it is more prudent to use instead the expression "sense" or "contextual sense." Without a minimal element of sense or meaning, without at least the attempt to find references from one thing to another, without direction (and sense is direction, reference to . . . , possibility of connection), there is no human life.

That everything must have its condition, some condition or other, does not imply the demand for a universal causality or teleology, but the expectation of continuities and references in terms of which man adapts himself to something *as* that in terms of which it is addressable, interrogable, controllable: in a word, as what he takes it as. A landscape, for example, can be taken as land for building, recreational area, strategic problem, object of agricultural science, site of industry, or as an aesthetic object, i.e., it can be understood, interrogated, and responded to in this or that "sense." It can fulfill or disappoint our expectations in this or that direction, but in some direction or other there must be something "to be done with it." (Personal talents do not count here.) For the rest, we may leave open the question, how far that aspect of sense or meaning is bound to contexts of end, value, or being. For what follows, it is enough to have thrown into relief a basic tendency of human existence, to which the analysis of laughter, and, indeed, of laughter alone, has already led us.

What occasions or situations excite us to laugh? Generally speaking, those which are not serious, or which are not taken seriously. Seriousness is intended here in a dual sense: in the sense of ordinary responsiveness on the basis of some condition or other, as well as in the sense of an extraordinary threat, on the basis of some overwhelming danger. Whenever we are threatened by some danger to body, mind, or spirit, laughter is repressed unless we have the power to disregard it, remove ourselves from it, or in some measure take it into account. This possibility of the humorous objectification of our own annihilation is open to us on principle. Then the situation becomes hopeless for us, but not serious.*

Unanswerable situations, in which man cannot orient himself, to which he can find no relation, whose condition he cannot discover, which he cannot understand and cannot grasp: with which, therefore, he can do nothing, are equally intolerable. He will try at any price to change them, to transform them into situations "answerable" in some way or other, or to escape them. If he does not succeed, such situations can grow to become threats to his existence; in whatever respect, in his sensuous and bodily existence, in his affective life, or at the intellectual level, things become serious; he will lose his head, and a crisis will ensue. But if the unanswerable situation does not hold him fast, then he will retreat from it without expenditure of energy.

Why does a condition or occasion which is in no sense serious or to be taken seriously, which neither has a threatening character in itself nor is in any way associated with one—why does such a state of affairs make us laugh? If it did not hold us fast, did not positively bind us, then we could free ourselves from it without expenditure of energy, and the explosive reaction of laughter would remain incomprehensible. A certain energy is necessary, because a state of not being serious makes itself felt only *contrary* to all expectation. Contrary to all expectation, i.e., with the illusion of seriousness. This illusion of the threatening or of the normal does not dwindle away to nothing but remains preserved in the transparency of a multiplicity of sense.

* There was a well-known saying in World War I: "Die Lage ist hoffnungslos—aber nicht ernst."—M. G.

Thus the situation does not become too much for the person involved, and yet holds him fast. He cannot free himself from it without difficulty, but is kept in tension through the entwinement or intersection of attracting and repelling aspects, i.e., aspects in which it is possible to enter into the situation and to respond to it, and aspects with the opposite character. Situations like titillation, play, comedy, wit, or embarrassment reveal in their ambivalence, ambiguity, and multiplicity of meaning the antagonism between binding and repulsion, answerableness and unanswerableness, and in such a way that the binding and repelling factors characterize the particular occasion, not in different aspects, but in the same. The conditions which exclude our responding to and entering into the situation (i.e., as an unambiguous context) at the same time determine their binding, uniting power. In this "at the same time," in the entwinement, intersection, and reciprocal transparency, lies the source of amusement.

Unanswerableness, through (various) mutually exclusive possibilities of response, sets up resistance against a rebuff by the problematical situation, i.e., the tension which is released in laughter. Thus we respond to the unanswerable in its multiplicity of sense. Thus we put "paid" to a situation which is vitally, spiritually, and existentially "contrary" to sense (which does not dwindle away to nothing, like the simply contradictory or the purely senseless, but unfolds its "sense in nonsense" in irresolubly oscillating tension, in meaningful transparency) with a reaction which betrays at one and the same time both self-assertion and self-abandonment. When a man laughs, he gives way to his own body and thus foregoes unity with it and control over it. With this capitulation as a unity of ensouled body and mind, he asserts himself as a person. The body, fallen out of relation to the person, takes over the answer for him, no longer as an instrument for acting, speaking, gesturing, or posturing but in direct counteraction. In the loss of control over his body, in disorganization, man still gives evidence of his sovereignty in an impossible situation. In this situation, he is disrupted as an ordered unity of mind, soul, and body, but this disruption is the last card he plays. In sinking below his level of controlled, or at least articulated, corporeality, he directly demonstrates his humanity: to be able to deal with something at the point where nothing further can be done.

b) What basic characteristic of the normal human situation must be called into question if man is to be able to cry? In crying, too, man provides an answer by giving way to an anonymous automatism. Only, in contrast to laughter, he implicates himself in the answer. Moved, stirred, shaken, inwardly concerned—not only irritated, amused, fascinated, surprised, i.e., taken out of himself (as in the occasion of laughter)—he lets *himself* go, so that he can cry. Letting oneself be overcome is the releasing and constitutive motive of weeping. Man capitulates—before a superior force with which he can no longer cope. Even in this respect, the situation of the person who cries formally resembles that of the person who laughs: behavior comes up against a barrier to all determinations of condition, before which word and deed, gesture and expressive movement, fail to be effective. He falls into an unanswerable situation.

What is decisive, however, is the locus of this unanswerableness. It is amusing if it is engendered by an irreconcilable multiplicity of sense, by an entwining, intersecting, mutually transparent nexus of relations of meaning. This structure makes for lack of seriousness. With crying, on the other hand, the helplessness results from a curious immediacy in the exposure to pain, in the sudden shift from tenseness to relaxation, and in being deeply moved. Now "helplessness," by its very meaning, can have the appearance of being only a matter of the inability to resist a force. Such may seem to be the case in situations involving physical and mental pain. On the other hand, in peripeteia, in remorse, overpowering joy, conversion, and in the various forms of being deeply moved, helplessness appears as an absence of distance—not from the actual feeling but from the content which engrosses me in the feeling, which rouses and shakes me. Being moved emotionally, whether by the sublime and the powerful or the tender and the infirm, is to encounter the thing itself without mediation. Our behavior, oriented to relations and the relative, here comes to an absolute end. Basically, the same state of affairs prevails in the forms of peripeteia: they place man between two finalities in the irreversible stream of time. They throw him back upon his own finitude in the irretrievability of lived existence.

In the disruption of the normal relativity of our existence in and with the world, which usually conceals from us the clarity of Being, we arrive at a boundary of all behavior. Whatever power constitutes this boundary, whether destructive pain or relaxing joy, forgiving grace or quiet rapture, it always occurs as an unconditioned end in unmediated proximity. The encounter with such power creates a state of affairs with which man can do just as little as he can with an amusing situation. If there is in the latter case a complex intersectional structure which holds one in tension without making possible a discharge in one of the many possible lines of behavior, there is in the former a complete lack of complexity and an immediacy of interpenetration by emotion which thwarts all behavior.

Human existence needs elbowroom in order to develop. It has to react, to link up with, to respond. This free space can be taken from an individual through a direct threat to his physical, affective, or mental existence. Then he finds himself confronted by death. It can also be taken from him—thus forcing him against a barrier—by the blocking of every determinable condition, by the irremediable ambiguity of every cue to action, or by the negation of the relativity of existence. Then nothing remains for him but to give to such impossible situations the correspondingly impossible answers: to laugh or cry. And just as it is man's prerogative to get into such impossible situations—impossible for him as a person, but unavoidable for his intellectual nature, i.e., his eccentricity—so it is also his prerogative to let his body answer in his place.

To be sure, from the factors just discussed, we still cannot understand why the reaction to the thwarting of behavior through the irremediable ambiguity of all cues to action is precisely laughter (and not crying), while the reaction to the negation of the relativity of existence is precisely crying (and not laughter). But it does explain the connection of laughing and crying, their inner relationship and their antagonism.

2. The Two Boundary Reactions

One thing at least the analysis has established: what is reflected in the contrast of laughing and crying is not the superficial duality of joy and sorrow, pleasure and pain, but a twofold limitation of human behavior as such. As reactions to a boundary situation they reveal typical common properties which, to be sure, cause difficulties for the interpretation of their differences.[28] If they were modes of expressive movement like the expressions of emotion, if they were gestures, then their expressive patterns would be transparent. But as expressions of a disorganization in the relation of the person to his body, a disorganization which is a response to the onset of an impossibility of behavior, they must be, on the contrary, opaque. If our thesis is correct, there is no further way to make them "intelligible."

Thus with a good conscience our analysis could really hand over to physiology the question of why the reaction to the thwarting of behavior by the irremediable ambiguity of cues to action is precisely laughter, and to the thwarting of behavior by negation of relativity is precisely crying. Where intelligibility and explicability leave off, causal analysis can always try its luck. Why should it not be possible for such an analysis to clarify the mechanism of laughing and crying, a mechanism which comes into play under the conditions recognized by our analysis, even though its explanation exceeds our competence?

Naturally, such an outcome, if not wholly to the discredit of philosophy, would still be disappointing in its main thesis. The defeatists, who had held from the beginning that the question of the origin of laughing and crying admits of no solution, could triumph and declare that "at bottom" we still had made no headway. It would still be possible to ask only about the "how" and not about the "why." To be sure, the analysis would have clarified the conditions under which laughing and crying come into existence (conditions of the possibility of being able to laugh and cry), and it would have succeeded in making intelligible to what extent there are not merely one but two modes of expressing disorganization. But still it would not have succeeded in finding the relation of the forms of expression themselves from the motivation of their duality. Indeed, as if to justify this lack of success, the undertaking would reassure itself by its thesis of the manifest impenetrability of the expressive form in this case, and thus would even make a victory out of its failure.

But the defeatists triumph too soon. Even if there does exist a limit of transparency and intelligibility, this is not to say that we have already run up against it here. The boundary between the conditions under which laughing and crying as modes of disorganization can occur in a significant and intelligible way and the actual manner of their occurrence as laughing or as crying need not coincide with that limit. In fact, many relations prevail between the intelligible conditions and the actual form of expression. The physical expressions of laughing and crying can truly be appropriate to the occasion and react to its "sense" without—as holds true of expressive movement—being molded by it.

Openness, immediacy, eruptivity characterize laughter; closure, mediacy, gradualness characterize crying. These characteristics are not accidental. The laughing person is open to the world. In consciousness of our withdrawal and disengagement, which can frequently be combined with a feeling of superiority, we seek to know that we are one with others. Laughter succeeds completely only in company with those who laugh with us.

Why? The occasion of laughter, hence the onset of a thwarting of behavior through the irremediable ambiguity of cues to action, has an effect which is all the more pronounced, the more "objective" it seems. And it seems more objective to the degree that others are also struck by it. To that extent it requires endorsement by others and gains strength in community. Of like significance is the fact that the laughing person first becomes truly joyous in his laughter if others join in with him, that his laughter rings out and would be heard—for which exhalation is the appropriate means.

Immediacy and eruptivity are just as closely bound to the structure of the specific occasion. A person is not gradually subjected to the thwarting of behavior by the irremediable ambiguity of cues to action, nor does he experience this as a growing insistence, emotion, and revulsion of mood, but suddenly, unexpectedly, on the recoil and rebound. Naturally, laughter also undergoes a development, internal as well as external. Only this development takes a shorter time than that of crying. Above all, laughter tends to conclude its "ascent" quickly and merge into the actual outburst. Crying, on the other hand, has a tendency to become stationary, even though (if it does not lead to squalling, wailing, or moaning) it does describe a curve: growth, culmination, exhaustion. In the running-off of the expression of laughter, the immediacy and eruptivity characteristic of it suppress the character of development and of decrease because their reactive sense so requires it. Lability and suddenness are simply part of the occasion of laughter. Thus it is also related to the sounds of surprise and alarm. Nor should we exclude the possibility that from the study of respiratory shock reactions,[29] in particular, we may also acquire knowledge of the mechanism of laughter.

Language has a good expression for the status of crying: to be touched. Included in this expression is the connection of the relaxation of tension with the rise of emotion. In the act of inner capitulation which has a significance for crying at once evocative and constitutive, the individual becomes detached, in the sense of being isolated, from the situation of normal behavior. Deeply moved, he implicates himself by this act in the anonymous "answer" of his body. Thus in weeping he cuts himself off from the world.

Why? The occasion of crying in the thwarting of behavior through the negation of the relativity of existence has an effect which is the more pronounced, the more "subjectively," with the greater inner resonance, it takes possession of the individual. Here the fact that others are also moved must have an inhibitory effect on crying.

Must—not can? In primitive societies, whose members have a weaker consciousness of individuality, and in the spontaneous mass emotions of our highly civilized mass-world, the converse is also possible. Lowering of personal standards and the blurring of boundaries between individuals make the latter susceptible to "group emotions" and collective reactions, which occur so characteristically with monkeys, for example. Human beings remain always exposed to such danger of contagion, with the corresponding suppression of inhibition in all phases of their expressional life—in crying just as much as in laughing. But this collective laughing or crying is brought about externally through mass seizure; it has no true primality, nor has it attained the true dimensions of laughing and crying. The more developed man is, the more reserved will he be in his efforts to hide his tears. And all the more sparing will he be of them, for all the more precious to him will be the moment in which he is at liberty to yield to them.

As deep emotion, closure, and mediacy belong together, so do mediacy and gradualness of development of expression, so do deep emotion and weakening. The modes of unrelatedness do not take us by surprise. Even if we are "suddenly" overcome, feeling, emotion, and shock must first develop into loss of self-control. Corresponding to it is muscular flaccidity (e.g., trembling of the lower lip), the welling-up of tears which blur vision, sighing, which is accentuated by inhalation, as if in expression of estrangement from the world and of isolation.

For laughing and crying, therefore, connections can be established between the releasing motive or boundary situation in behavior and the physical mode of expression. In their status, they suit the occasion, they "answer" to it, although without being stamped by its significance as in the case of expressive movement. They receive their stamp through an automatism withdrawn from the control of the person to which it yields—yields "fittingly," to be sure. And here the boundary between the intelligible and unintelligible parts of the reaction comes to light. How is it possible that disorganization, which understandably points now in the direction of laughter, now of crying, has at its disposal two separate mechanisms which only rarely become confused? How is it possible that man, precisely as an intellectual being, *can* lose his relation to his own body in so characteristic a way?

Again, there are two things which must be distinguished in this question. On the one hand, there is the matter of the possibility of a sudden change to an autonomous reaction of the body as such. This possibility may be understood if, instead of the obscure and schematic ideas of the connection of mind and body conceived under the influence of metaphysical doctrines, the relation of man to his body, i.e., his eccentric position, forms the foundation. On the other hand, there is the matter of the participation of definite physiological mechanisms with whose aid the sudden change from personal existence in and with a living body to existence as a physical body takes place. The study of such mechanisms is the business of physiology. If our study has already declared from the beginning that the task of comprehending laughing and crying from the human point of view, in the original concreteness of our existence, as bodily reactions, can no more be undertaken by physiology than by psychology, or by the bilateral discipline of psychophysics, then the corollary must now be added: except for the study of the mechanisms which come into play with laughing and crying. But, on the other hand, the fact of the participation of *some* mechanism or other, i.e., the sudden change itself, can be understood only from the perspective of the whole man.

Bodily existence forces on man a dual role. *At one and the same time,* he *is* his body and *in* or *with* a body. In expressing this being-with and being-in, we also say: we have a (living) body. Being and having continuously shade off into each other in the fulfillment of existence, just as they are entwined with each other. At one time the human person confronts his body as an instrument, at another he coincides with it and is a body. Wherever it is a question of the control of the bodily mechanisms, in acting and speaking, in using signs, in gestures and expressive movements, we experience the ambiguity of physical existence. The relation between man (as person, as bearer of responsibility, subject of will, or however the predicates of his mental nature may be expressed) and his body fluctuates—and must fluctuate—between having and being.

To want to come to a decision between the two modes of existence "as living body" and as "in a living body," as if there were an alternative, would be to misunderstand their reciprocal entwinement. Without the certainty of my own inner location in my body, there would be no certainty of the immediate exposure of myself as body to the effects and countereffects of other bodily things. And conversely: without the certainty of the externality of myself as body in the space of bodily things, there would be no certainty of my being myself within my living body, i.e., no control of my own physical body, no synchronization of its movements with the environment, no "true apprehension" of the environment. The one is inseparable from the other; one conditions the other, as it is conditioned by it. With the same justification, every individual holds fast to the absolute reference of the environment to his body or to the center of perception, thinking, willing (i.e., to his "I"), persisting "in" it, just as, in turn, he abandons this reference in favor of the mutual interrelation of all things with one another, including his body (and therewith the "I"). This position of being at once in the middle and on the periphery deserves the name of eccentricity.

Man must constantly find a relation to this eccentricity, since his nature is exhausted neither by the mid-point position alone (being "in" the body, or having it) nor by the peripheral position alone (being the body itself). Every requirement of his existence demands an accommodation between the mode of being and the mode of having. The mediated, instrumental, and expressive character of his existence is disclosed and achieved for him in the compulsion to find an accommodation between the physical thing that he happens to be and the living body in which he dwells and which he controls. This body, then, is to him:

1. Means, tool, organ for the execution of all movements, but at the same time a constraint on them which it is necessary to surmount. On this account, with the exception of certain au-

tonomic functions (partly of a reflex nature), physical existence must be learned by man, in order—though mediated—to become immediate. Thus, the body is to us:

2. Material, reflective surface, sounding board for the different modes of expression, speech, gesture, and expressive movement.

In order for a man to utilize his body instrumentally or expressively, in accordance with some circumstances or other, there must be a demand addressed to him which either can or cannot be satisfied. For those demands which can be satisfied, action and speech, gesture and expressive movement suffice. For those which cannot be satisfied, they fail. But what if a situation breaks out of this frame of reference? In such situations, with which we no longer know how to deal, we necessarily lose the referent in terms of which we could find a relation to our physical existence. The direction is missing in which we must organize ourselves into the unity of the person with and in our bodily existence. With the disappearance of this referent for accommodation between being and having a body, disorganization is at hand: the two modes split immediately apart, the body emancipates itself as the instrument and sounding board of the person. Automatism in some form or other comes into play for the man who, as a person dominating and controlling his entire existence, is played out.

Up to this limit, the origin of laughing and crying may be clarified. On the other hand, the study of the means by which the sudden change to automatism takes place remains the business of physiology. Nothing certain is yet known of this. Clues, perhaps, may be found in the phenomena of compulsive laughing and crying with pseudobulbar paralysis,[30] in the initial stage of schizophrenia, in the dry sobbing of severe depression, and in similar pathological phenomena. But such inferences from the pathological to the normal case are never unobjectionable. As soon as the motivation of the reaction is removed, the reactive character of the compulsive processes which seem to resemble laughing and crying also becomes questionable. Besides: is similarity in appearance sufficient to warrant an inference to similarity in origin?

It would be possible—indeed, on the basis of observations which everyone has made both in himself and others under circumstances of extreme fatigue and overstimulation, also in such vital crises as puberty, for example, it is even probable—that both the physical causes of laughing and crying and their actual mechanism can vary. The existence of localizable sensitive areas in the brain, the so-called centers, whose excitation brings the mechanism in question into play, remains open in any case, so that a critical physiology cannot base itself on a program of centers in this area either.

It might be—and the diversity of the habitual patterns of laughing and crying favors this supposition—that the two reactions belong to different functional systems, to the animal and the vegetative, respectively, whose opposition pervades the entire organism. Pointing toward this conclusion is the pronounced state of muscular tension in laughter, whose occasions are found in the region of ideational life, and the relaxed state of the musculature, along with a hyperactivity of certain glands, in crying, which is released by feeling. Such an antagonism would conform just as much to the contrast of the relevant mental inducements as to that of the physical functions. And it is an attractive idea to bring both the reactions that occur at the limits of behavior into connection with each other, not only with regard to the two systems of animal and vegetative functions, which directly complement each other, but also with regard to the opposition of consciousness and feeling. In this way, even disorganization would reveal itself as organized.[31] Neither the fact that we may make a wrong choice of expression, nor that there can be a sudden transition from laughing to crying or crying to laughing, nor, for that matter, the fact that in the development of the two reactions there are common traits: none of these facts contradicts the idea of the basic antagonism.

Too good to be true? We cannot yet say for sure. Only one thing is certain: whatever the physical connections may be, they are not immaterial to our knowledge of the relation of a man to his body and to the world. If man, even as body, is a being capable of mental life, a being who has a relation to his body and the world, then the means which permit him to have these relations, and, with them, mind, must be adapted to that end. Otherwise, must we not assume that leading a mental existence is equivalent to—living beyond one's means?

That laughing and crying are contrasting phenomena is instinctively clear to everyone, but the popular interpretation of this contrast has always allowed itself to be overly influenced by the ordinary view of life. For the most part, says popular opinion, men laugh because they are amused and cry because they are sorrowful. But amusement and sorrow, pleasure and pain, are opposites too crude for the richness of life. The equation "laughter = pleasure" may still balance after a fashion, but the equation "crying = pain" is surely false.

If the pleasure principle thus breaks down with regard to laughing and crying, what then gives assurance of their contrariety? On this point, our analysis replies: *their character as reactions to a crisis of human behavior as such.* Contrast is possible only between things which share common features. What is common to laughing and crying is that they are answers to a *boundary situation.* Their opposition depends on the mutually contrasted directions in which man falls into this boundary situation. Since it makes itself known as a boundary situation only in the twofold way in which every possible mode of human behavior is blocked or thwarted, there are only two crisis reactions having the character of a response to such a situation. Laughter responds to the thwarting of behavior by the irremediable ambiguity of cues to action, crying to the thwarting of behavior by the negation of the relativity of human existence.

Vital behavior takes place between the living being which conducts itself actively or passively, rationally or irrationally, skillfully or awkwardly, etc., *and* that which confronts it. The suppression of behavior in this sense can therefore be attributed (assuming complete insight into the interweaving of both components) only to the living being which embodies this behavior or to what confronts it. Each such blockage limits and finally threatens life. The living being is exposed to this process through its weakness. Under certain circumstances it leads to disturbances of function and to illness, and it is terminated by death. As a living being, man is subject to the law of this kind of suppression.

Beyond this, however, specifically human behavior has yet another dimension, within which it takes place and in which it can come up against *boundaries.* This dimension stamps man with the seal of indirectness and mediacy. In everything in which he holds himself superior to animals, man stands *between* himself, the subject of behavior, and its objects. Thus he can dispose of himself and them—or blunder. This indirectness and mediacy reveals itself in man's attentiveness to *relations:* both in the world (himself included) and *between* the world and himself. His behavior does not (or does not only) take place in conformity with the relations prevailing at the moment, but as *confronting* them, in altercation with them. Animals behave according to the situation, follow its relationships (more or less), adapt to them or perish by them; man sees them and conducts himself in the consciousness of their organization—he articulates them: through language, through schematic projects for action and for shaping. He not only masters these relations, he also understands them *as* relations and can isolate the relation as such from the concrete situation. He must take them in some *sense* or other: concretely or paradigmatically, practically or contemplatively.

Thus the space in which he could act can also be closed off, if conditions for the formation of relations as such are disturbed. Vitally everything remains in order, but with the *state of affairs* "in this or that sense" it is all over. A phenomenon that he observes, the way he feels, a remark that he understands, suddenly affords no further cue to action. Things have got out of all relation to one another, and thus he can discover no relation to them. He no longer knows how to "relate" to them and to himself.

As we have said, then: the conditions for the formation of relations as such are in every sense disturbed, so that connections within the world and to the world are no longer possible: no allusions, clues, points of contact, no comparisons or distinctions. This again can happen in two ways. For the suppression of relationships signifies the suppression of every possibility of sense and comprehension of sense. This can *either* be attained by contradictory meanings, which suspend all univocality, *or* by the erasure of every mediating relation, the annihilation of the relativity of human life, which makes any attempt at interpretation impossible. In the one case, behavior is prohibited by the irremediable ambiguity of the cues to action (in play, in the phenomenon of the comic, in wit and humor, in embarrassment and despair). In the other case, it is prohibited by negation of the relativity of existence (in the modes of being moved and shaken, of capitulation and self-abandonment before and to the "facts" in the resonant appeal of feeling).

The suppression of behavior in these two mutually opposed cases is naturally not to be understood as if man were here condemned to passivity.

Passivity too is a mode of behavior; whether it is suitable or not depends on the situation and its particular significance. Behavior in play even shows, in connection with the object of play, activity adequate to the meaning of the situation, activity which can exhibit the highest degree of perfection but which as such still embodies an indissoluble ambiguity of the cues to action. This ambiguity—if it emerges from the sphere of vital processes (and the player can bring this about at any time: it spices the play and brings him the full enjoyment of his freedom)—evokes laughter.

What is suppressed here is the possible *univocality* to which all serious behavior is oriented (insofar as it is meant to be taken seriously—and this applies not only to prosaic and businesslike behavior, which is rational in the narrow sense of conforming to logic, but also to religious, artistic, or moral behavior, which is justified by a value and is molded in accordance with it).

In this context, therefore, the term "univocality" should not be limited to statements. All behavior has its own kind of univocality, the scientific as well as the political, the artistic, or the religious. This univocality can become a mask if the underlying intention is different: science can serve as a mask for political expediency, religious worship as a mask for aesthetic experience. Even such equivocal, ambiguous behavior, with its opacity or transparency, is serious if it follows *one* course and stresses only one of the two spheres of significance. It becomes frivolous and can form a source of amusing collisions if it tries to serve both masters. But the intersection of spheres of value need by no means always be involved in order to give rise to an amusing equivocation through the irremediable ambiguity of cues. As the analysis of the occasions of laughter has shown, it can be attained with like precision within a single sphere of significance (or of value).

Univocality or literal meaning is distinguished not only from ambiguity and multiplicity of meaning but also from emptiness of meaning and significance. Language, the medium of understanding and of life, has no word for this. Language discovers and founds relations, allusions, and connections and wards off what is hostile to them (such as the nonsensical, the senseless, and the absurd). Now it would be wise to distinguish here between something which makes a nexus of sense impossible because it is not in accord with the conditions of that nexus (e.g., logically, because it violates the principle of identity, linguistically, because it violates the rules of sentence formation by using meaningless signs or by not paying attention to the possibilities and limitations of a given sphere of meaning: perhaps using artistic arguments in a lawsuit, moral arguments in a scientific dispute, and so on) and what in general does not enter into *any* nexus of sense or reference. Only the latter is sense-free and can be encountered only immediately through feeling. Hence there are no intellectual criteria for it. Furthermore, whether such a thing moves a person, grips him, and compels him to capitulate, whether he encounters it in such a way that it is detached from all reference, in genuine freedom from sense, depends exclusively on him and not on what happens to him externally.

However, we claim neither an ontological nor an axiological priority for such encounters. Nor do we claim for a specific subject matter of a transcendental character a privileged use or monopoly of this moving, shaking, or touching effect. Empirical things, rational contexts, and values can also come upon a person in this way and therewith become detached from every possibility of reference and connection. The psychic "conditions" for such a contact are beside the point here; nor need we stress the fact that many types are inclined toward such contact, and others not, that certain moods, situations, and, naturally, particular subject matters (e.g., phenomena of a religious or artistic kind) encourage it. It is a matter of the contact itself, of its intrinsic effect: a pervasive reattunement which transforms and overpowers.

Univocality of reference is not clarity or certainty of belief *about* the sense concerned. Also, it would be absurd to think that univocality is limited in conformity with rational criteria. On the contrary, it applies in all realms or spheres of significance, theoretical as well as practical, in everyday life as well as in the relation of man to God, in science as well as in art, in active as well as in contemplative behavior. It applies even in the realm of the aesthetic, with its openness of reference through imagery, poetry, melody, and sustains the appropriate conduct. Openness, i.e., the unspecifiable, inexpressible, indescribable nature of aesthetic meaning, is itself a kind of univocality, the contrary, not of the univocal, but of the closed character of other modes of sense and relation. The beauty, the profundity, the richness of content and meaning of an aesthetic impression, whether in nature or art, inexhaustible secret for a perceptive and listening heart: this is the univocality of the aesthetic sphere. It, too, like all other regions of human conduct, is delimited in two ways: through the irremediable ambiguity of its references and through the negation of relativity in the whole.

In order to grasp this double delimitation, we must bear in mind the unique nature of human behavior. We said: behavior as such works between a living being and its opposite in such a way that the two, subject and object, enter into connection. Whatever the goal of the behavior may be, and whether it is realized or not, in every case it brings about a connection between the living being and its opposite. With man, however, behavior seems to be mediated. That is, although even here behavior brings about an immediate contact, in this case it is mediated by the subject of the behavior, which is conscious of itself insofar as it is a subject in and over against certain objective relations. Thus, at the very least, man *can* (within definite, though sometimes extendable, limits) have command over himself and his objects; thus, he conducts himself by virtue of indirectness and mediacy within the framework of relations and in conformity with their criteria. For someone to be conscious of himself means being able to insert himself into the connection between himself and his "opposite." Such behavior is not simply immediate, but mediated in all its immediacy. It takes place within the framework of relations, i.e., references, cues to action, and connotations.

All human immediacy, insofar as it is specifically human, insofar as it holds out against impulse and instinct through individual relations to others and to the world (always with difficulty, always threatened by misunderstanding), is mediated. This many-leveled structure of behavior is clear to man himself; it harasses him constantly with problems of an intellectual, technical, volitional, and emotional kind. As soon as he leaves the narrow circle of the familiar and the commonplace, he must discover connections of meaning, of "relations." He must always first determine the makeup of this or that circumstance. Mediated immediacy, therefore, necessarily moves *on the boundary between sense and not-sense* [*Nicht-Sinn*], a boundary, as we said, displaceable in various ways and separating the sphere of the intelligible from the not yet intelligible. But for this reason human behavior also has the prospect of coming up against boundaries of the not-sensical which are no longer displaceable, i.e., boundaries of an essential kind. They turn out to be beyond the possible for human behavior, and man, its bearer, then responds to the situation with laughing or crying: with laughing to the limitation arising from ambiguity of cues, with crying to the limitation arising from the loss of reference through negation of the relativity of human existence as a whole.

If the one kind of limitation must be presented, in the form of a relinquishment of binding connections, as dissociation [*Loslösung*] (in play, the comic, wit and humor, embarrassment and despair), then the other kind must be presented in the form of an encounter with the dissociated as the immediately affecting (the moving, shaking, transforming, undoing, overpowering). Both kinds of limitation lie (*ex definitione*) outside the sphere of competence of the rational and occur as disruptions of those relations which are binding for reason and volition. Thus we can understand why the occasions of laughing and crying have traditionally been treated in aesthetics and why laughing and crying themselves are regarded as aesthetic modes of behavior. Admittedly, this fact, along with the prejudice that insists on a dominant role in aesthetics for the concepts of beauty and ugliness, has caused a good deal of confusion. The reverse of this procedure would be more nearly correct. Our insight into the nature and extent of the aesthetic can succeed only if it is oriented to human behavior—a world till now much talked about but practically undiscovered. The theory of human behavior has remained hitherto in the shadow of classical philosophy and has taken its guiding principles from the normative sciences.

For the knowledge of human nature, this procedure has been emphatically disadvantageous. As certain as it is that man's nature can be fulfilled only in reference to his vocation, so far is that nature from being exhausted by such a reference. The fact remains that man is always more or less than his true vocation: in Herder's words, an invalid of his own spiritual powers. Even such body-bound expressions as laughing and crying can be understood only out of this honorable disproportion in his nature.

Notes and References

1. *Die Einheit der Sinne. Grundlinien einer Aesthesiologie des Geistes* (Bonn, 1923; reprinted 1964).

2. *Die Stufen des Organischen und der Mensch. Einleitung in die Philosophische Anthropologie* (Berlin, 1928; 2nd ed., 1956).

3. The opinion that animals can laugh (and cry) has adherents not only among laymen. Developmental and animal psychologists as well occasionally side with this view. Their arguments, however (see, e.g., C. W. Dix, *Das Seelenleben des Kindes im ersten Lebensjahr* [Jena, 1939]), are purely of an external nature. Doubtless there occur —above all in species zoologically related to man, but certainly not only in such species and surely also in young children (see R. W. Washburn, "A Study of Smiling and Laughing in the First Year of Life," *Genetic Psychology Monographs*, VI [1929], 5–6)—expressions of enjoyment, titillation, discomfort, and pain which, in outward manifestation, match or are similar to laughing and crying. The sounds of tittering or of giggling, baying and howling, the drawing-wide of the mouth, the narrowing of the eyelids, the flow of tears, and similar phenomena in corresponding situations seem to strengthen the view in question. Those who dispute this notion, i.e., by reference to the fully developed meaning in which the words *laughing* and *crying* are used in the human sphere, expose themselves to the suspicion of making man the measure and of making our concept of laughing and crying an absolute, thus anthropomorphizing these concepts and so cutting off in advance discussion of the question whether laughing and crying occur in infants and animals.

This is not how the matter lies. In fact, laughing and crying are concepts which are taken from human behavior. They must first be explained in their original sphere of application before they can serve as designations of extrahuman or of primitive human behavior. The establishment of formal similarities in conduct between animals and men (who *know* that they laugh and cry) is not a sufficient foundation on which to base the conclusion that animals can also laugh and cry. To do this, one must first determine the significance of the region in which the formal similarity lies. First comes the question, what part the mode of expression plays in the behavior characterized as laughing and crying, and this question depends in turn on the relation of the subject stimulated to his particular form of expression. Only because we know that the mode of expression in the pantomime of the *affects* rests on a purely biological form of expression of the excited "internal state" may we admit the corresponding expressive movements of animals and infants in corresponding situations as expressive movements of joy, fear, rage, etc. And since the supposition naturally suggests itself that with laughing and crying it is likewise a question of affective gestures, some people trust to the formal similarity of the range of expression in both animals and men and come to the conclusion that animals can also laugh and cry. This conclusion is wrong because the supposition is wrong, as our analysis demonstrates.

Our analysis does not make an absolute of the human concept of laughing and crying but takes this concept only as a starting point. That overscrupulousness and pseudo-exactitude which would eliminate everything subjective and in need of interpretation in order to arrive at purely objective results necessarily fails to come to grips with a problem like that of laughing and crying. What can be established about the modes of expression in question by the use of recording techniques which objectify what they record is certainly of value for the knowledge of the underlying physiological conditions. But the analysis of the modes of expression on the whole can neither begin with nor be limited to such techniques.

4. Thus, e.g., for H. W. McComas, "The Origin of Laughter," *Psych. Rev.*, XXX (1923), laughter is an instinctive mode of behavior in connection with pleasurable experience, which later becomes detached through pleasurable impressions, through other instincts, and through determinate trains of thought and finally often takes the place of speech. In primitive times, laughter replaced speech in the sense of an invitation to continue actions that one expected to be accompanied by pleasure, or to participate in the enjoyment. D. Hayworth, "The Social Origin and Function of Laughter," *Psych. Rev.*, XXXV (1928), sees in laughter a signal to the other members of the group that relaxation without danger is possible. In reliance on McDougall's social psychology, Gopalaswami ("The Genesis of the Laughter Instinct," *Psychological Studies,* University of Mysore, 1926) seeks the solution in a similar direction. The influence of Bergson and Freud, however, has contributed essentially to the refinement of the analysis. The work of S. H. Bliss, "The Origin of Laughter," *Amer. Jour. Psych.*, XXVI (1915), shows this also. His study, proceeding from the conflict between natural and social drives, sees in laughter the outcome of abruptly canceled repression, the physical token of subconscious satisfaction. Anglo-American interest in the question and its history (Sully, Eastman, Gregory), moreover, remains striking. A comparison with its neglect by German psychology

and philosophy of the past decades shows, at any rate, that those whose native tongue is English can philosophize without losing their sense of humor.

5. Thus, not only existential philosophers, but also theorists concerned with expression as well as anthropologists, believe that they can dismiss the problem of the relation of mind and body. "It is superfluous, so to speak, for we have a third standpoint," says A. Gehlen (*Der Mensch,* [Berlin, 1940; 7th ed., Frankfurt a.M., 1962]). Klages is not without guilt in this form of thoughtlessness, as one sees, e.g., in P. Helwig's *Seele als Äusserung* (Leipzig, 1936). Cf. also F. Gehrung, *Das Seelische. Wider die Verdoppelung des Menschen* (Berlin, 1938). K. Bühler in his *Ausdruckstheorie* (Jena, 1933) shows clearly, moreover, how strong the connection of the theory of expression is with expressive movement, gesture, speech, and action as sense-conveying and objectifying modes of expression.

6. For R. Reininger, *Das Psychophysische Problem. Eine erkenntnistheoretische Untersuchung zur Unterscheidung des Physischen und Psychischen überhaupt* [1916], roots of the mind-body problem lie "in the transitions from our own direct to our own indirect consciousness of the body."

7. Cf. H. von Kleist's story *Über das Marionettentheater.*

8. What face and voice signify in relation to expressivity, the hand signifies in relation to instrumentality: a controlling and representative organ, medium, and field. Herder-like problems! For this, see my book *Die Einheit der Sinne* (Bonn, 1923; reprinted 1964) and my article "Sensibilité et raison," *Recherches philosophiques* (1937). Further, H. Lipps' subtle observations in *Untersuchungen zu einer hermeneutischen Logik* (Frankfurt, 1938), esp. pp. 71 ff. and 109 ff. Also, F. J. J. Buytendijk, *Grondproblemen van het dierlijk leven* (Antwerp, 1938), esp. pp. 121 ff.

9. F. J. J. Buytendijk and H. Plessner, "Die Deutung des mimischen Ausdrucks," *Philosophischer Anzeiger,* I (1925).

10. See also H. Strehle, *Analyse des Gebarens* (Berlin, 1935). As late as the twenties works on the theory of expression could be counted on the fingers of one hand. Admittedly, today we have a series of monographs at our disposal (Ph. Lersch, *Gesicht und Seele* [Munich, 1932], K. Bühler, *op. cit.,* G. H. Fischer, *Ausdruck und Persönlichkeit* [Leipzig, 1934]). Even Jaensch's frenetic activity could not discredit this subject.

11. Hornbostel proved experimentally that these intermodal properties, i.e., properties not bound to one region or mode of sense, as, for example, clarity and dimness, permit associations between sensations of sight and hearing. These properties account for the singular phenomena of the mutual replaceability of modally different sensations and their ability to induce one another (synaesthesia). In the twenties, H. Werner and his students made the investigation of such phenomena their special task.

12. Ewald Hecker, *Die Physiologie und Psychologie des Lachens und des Komischen* (Berlin, 1873), devotes this detailed observation to the mechanism of tickling: "It is evident that the laughter arising

as a consequences of tickling, on the one hand . . . resting on a wise precaution of nature, fulfills definite material tasks; on the other hand, laughing at comic notions must also occur with the same necessity, since the comic with its (psychologically demonstrable) effect on our emotions evokes the same organic changes as tickling. The same is true of crying (or screaming) insofar as it arises through bodily pain and psychic feeling, and of yawning, insofar as it arises through bodily exhaustion and boredom" (p. 6). Hecker sees the same organic changes in the fluctuation of blood pressure in the brain, which in his opinion could become a danger for the normal functioning of that organ if the functional reflex of laughter, through its rhythmic expiratory movements, did not compensate for the fluctuations in pressure. Proceeding from the thesis that the intermittent skin stimulation of tickling results in an intermittent stimulation of the sympathetic nervous system and that this in turn has as a consequence an intermittent contraction of the vascular structure of the brain with corresponding fluctuations in the blood pressure of the brain, Hecker looked for an analogous structure in the "comic," the other releasing motive of laughter. He saw it in the synchronous release of pleasant and unpleasant feelings of like strength. Supported by the known phenomenon of the counteraction of visual fields and brightness—a very rapid counteraction—he believed himself justified in the statement (p. 80): "The comic is a mixed feeling of a peculiar kind; as is true with brightness, the individual components come into action in such quick succession that we have seemingly a homogeneous feeling before us." He thus obtains a connection with the Kant-Vischer theory of the nature of the laughable as a rapid fluctuation between pleasure and displeasure, so as finally to declare the comic (as the embodiment of the "laughable") to be an intermittent, rhythmically discontinuous, joyful excitation of feeling which—beginning unexpectedly—causes us to anticipate an intermittent stimulation of the sympathetic nervous system and so justifies the protective mechanism of laughter, as in the case of tickling.

There is no longer any difficulty in showing the untenability of the physiological and psychological bases of Hecker's theory. But in spite of this, it still merits our attention, for it tries at least to understand laughter as a reaction and to indicate the variety of the physical and mental possibilities of its evocation. If, in doing so, the theory makes the typical mistake of confusing the compulsive reaction to the tickling stimulus, i.e., tittering, with genuine laughter, it still sees the importance of the question of the releasing factors which obtain for all possibilities of evocation. To be sure, it provides too direct and contrived an answer to this question, but beyond this, its physiological interpretation of laughter as a protective reflex is worth examining and thinking about even today. Despite all the fundamental reservations about the interpretation of physiological functions as serviceable reflexes (laughter, in particular), in general, it is still better to bring the phenomenon within the compass of a meaningful context and to indicate some method or other of experimental verification than to rest content with its alleged unintelligibility. Cf. J. von Kries, "Vom Komischen und vom Lachen," *Arch. für Psychiatrie u. Nervenkrankheiten* (*Festschrift* for A. Hoche), pp. 241 ff.

13. Buytendijk's formulation in his *Het spel van mensch en dier als openbaring van levensdriften* (Amsterdam, 1932; German edition: *Wesen und Sinn des Spiels, Berlin,* 1933) is the best analysis of play we have.

14. *Widerstandsverlag* (Berlin, 1936).

15. S. Hochfeld, *Der Witz* (Potsdam and Leipzig, 1920). A confrontation with the literature which is missing in Jünger is found here in abundance. It is presented more distinctly in F. Jahn's *Das Problem des Komischen in seiner geschichtlichen Entwicklung* (Berlin, 1904).

16. André Jolles in *Einfache Formen* (Halle, 1929) treats jokes in this fashion.

17. From the *Frankfurter Zeitung* of August 13, 1938, No. 409.

18. Cf. K. Fischer, *Über den Witz,* Minor Works, 2d ed. (Stuttgart, 1889). Albert Wellek makes a fresh attempt to classify types of wit in "Zur Theorie und Phänomenologie des Witzes," *Studium Generale,* II (Berlin, 1949).

19. S. Freud, *Wit and Its Relation to the Unconscious, Collected Works,* Vol. VIII, trans. James Strachey (London, 1962).

20. Th. Reik (*Lust und Leid im Witz* [Vienna, 1929]) has further elaborated the Freudian theory. He finds the essence of joking in a twofold surprise. "We laugh as much over how a person says something as over what he says. The second effect is made possible through the first" (p. 101). This principle of the twofold surprise also holds true of the tendentious joke, since surprise in connection with wordplay represents the expression of astonishment over an unaccustomed freedom of thought and word usage, a source of pleasure which had been buried since childhood. This formal characteristic of facetious expressions, however, does not account for their full effect. It conditions only the so-called forepleasure, while the final pleasurable effect is conditioned by the content of the witty remark. Reik follows Freud here in holding that, on this point, formal aesthetics and psychology break down, above all when, appealing to Kant or Vischer, their adherents see the surprise in a joke as a disappointment, occurring through the sudden reduction of an expectation to nothing or its dissolution into something infinitely small. In fact, according to Reik, pleasure in the joke results from the sudden neutralization of the energy expended in inhibition. This inhibitory expenditure rests on the taboo of certain thoughts, ideas, and impulses, which are not to be allowed to come to consciousness, and the surprise reveals itself as a sudden recognition of something known of old, which had become unconscious. What is essential to the joke is not a disappointment, as the aestheticians decree, but precisely the confirmation of an unconscious expectation. The breakthrough brought about through the content of the facetious remark alarms the hearer and thus wakens in him the anxiety bound up with the primitive

taboo. "In a deeper sense than we first assumed, the surprise in the joke is thus a twofold one. It has the character of a double shock. The first surprise is based on the endopsychical perception of the unconscious emotional impulses, which succeed in coming to expression through the joke. The second is based on the emergence of that old anxiety of conscience, whose effect is the alarming thought. The sudden rush of impulse is followed just as suddenly by a reactive anxiety, as if it were a matter of a dangerous force. The mastering of this anxiety now deepens in an unforeseen way the satisfaction in the expression of the impulse which the joke presents. We begin to understand here how important the joke is, and hence how much stems from the pleasure in it, in particular, that we have crossed over an abyss, so to speak, with a whole skin. The idea dawns on us how very much all human pleasure is hemmed in by anxiety" (p. 112).

As far as the reaction of laughter is concerned, Reik takes over Freud's theory that the hearer of a joke laughs with the sum of psychic energy which has become free with the availability of the energy formerly possessed by the inhibition. For Reik, laughter is the expression of the manic mood which results from the mastery of anxiety and the free expression of impulse. Its effect is to be compared with the effect that terror has for the traumatic neurotic. "In trembling and in other symptoms, this terror subsequently masters the too-great rush of stimuli which have momentarily overwhelmed the psychical apparatus. While such neurotics exhibit excessive anxiety through their symptoms, they arrange for their disposal, as it were. They 'tremble them away'" (p. 113).

Doubtless, psychoanalytic theory represents an advance compared with explanations according to formal principles, such as bewilderment and enlightenment (Heymans) or damming-up and release (Lipps). Still, it seems to us that the appeal to a psychic reality which has become completely unconscious on occasion overshoots the mark. It is to be granted unconditionally that the power of the effect depends on the power of the tendency and the wealth of emotion associated with the matter to which the joke alludes. But the facetiousness itself does not depend on this, as Freud and Reik themselves, moreover, are at pains to emphasize. If, under the influence of psychoanalysis, one chooses to see the limitation of our outlook in this: that we restrict the effect of wit to the area of forepleasure, then we must rest content with this conclusion, without, of course, overlooking the essential significance of those areas of taboo which the joke so frequently breaks in upon. We are only challenging the notion that the form of the joke as such, as an occasion of laughter, is to be understood through the mechanics of displacement, and so on.

21. Out of the meager literature on this subject see W. Hellpach, "Vom Ausdruck der Verlegenheit. Ein Versuch zur Sozialpsychologie der Gemütsbewegungen," *Arch. f. d. ges. Psych.*, XXVII, Nos. 1 and 2 (1913), and H. J. F. W. Brugmans, "Die Verlegenheit, ihre Erscheinungen und ihr konstitutioneller Grund," *Zeitschr. f. Psych. u. Phys. d. Sinnesorgane*, I, Sec. LXXXI (1919).

22. Joh. Ed. Erdmann, *Über Lachen und Weinen* (Berlin, 1850), included in *Ernste Spiele* (1871).

23. A. Schopenhauer, *The World as Will and Idea,* Book Four, § 67, "On the Theory of the Ludicrous." Cf. the supplement to Book One, Chapter 8.

24. Ch. Spitz, *Zur Psychologie des Weinens,* doctoral dissertation, Leipzig, 1935. Unfortunately she did not take account of the work of B. Schwarz.

25. B. Schwarz, *Untersuchungen zur Psychologie des Weinens,* doctoral dissertation, Munich, 1928. It is instructive to compare the pertinent chapters on laughing and crying in G. Dumas's *Traité de Psychologie* (Paris, 1923–24), and also F. H. Lund, "Why Do We Weep?", *Social Psychology,* I (1930), 136–51, with Schwarz's study. Careful description of the phenomenon in its own element is too much neglected in these theories.

26. We meet here the difficult question of the so-called intentionality of feelings, whose classification also depends on its solution. Since the present context does not demand a decision on this question, we need not go into the considerable body of literature which has grown up in recent years. See in particular the work of Scheler, Geiger, Pfänder, K. Schneider, and the school represented by Felix Krueger (e.g., *Das Wesen der Gefühle* [Leipzig, 1928]). For the question of the resonant appeal see O. F. Bollnow, *Das Wesen der Stimmungen,* 2d ed. (Frankfurt am Main, 1943).

27. F. J. J. Buytendijk, *Reaktionszeit und Schlagfertigkeit* (Kassel, 1932).

28. The judgment that laughing and crying are reactions to boundary situations usually does not advance beyond the position of I. M. Willmann in "An Analysis of Humor and Laughter," *Amer. J. Psych.,* LIII, No. 1 (1940): "Laughter occurs when a total situation causes surprise, shock, or alarm and at the same time induces an antagonistic attitude of playfulness or indifference." He cites F. H. Lund, "Why Do We Weep?" *Soc. Psychol.,* I (1930): "Neither sorrow, dejection, joy, nor elation, when occurring in pure form, is very effective, if at all, in producing the lacrimal discharge. This discharge appears, typically, when a depressing or otherwise unpleasant situation acquires a redeeming feature or when tension and unpleasant stimulation are followed by pleasant or alleviating stimulation"; and he clarifies these views as follows: "While weeping is primarily associated with sorrow, apparently the situation most effective in producing actual tears is a double situation which creates sorrow and at the same time induces an opposite kind of response. It is in like manner that primary laughter is associated with joy and playfulness, as Darwin has pointed out, but that a playful appeal alone is not adequate to produce laughter (except in children). With adults the typical funny situation is one providing a playful appeal *plus* an antagonistic response to reinforce it." However, in the dual nature of the situation its character as a boundary is precisely revealed.

Gregory's observation in *The Nature of Laughter* (New York,

1924) also belongs here: "Laughter is *not* an act as a blow is an angry act or flight is a fearful act. Neither is it, properly speaking, an act of acceptance. The laughter simply holds its sides and laughs —its laughter is an action broken."

29. A more detailed investigation of the changes which respiratory motions undergo in laughing and crying provides a good starting point for the experimental analysis of laughing and crying. The conception of a graduated reduction of normal respiratory motions can be a guiding principle for the analysis. To what extent the assumption of a hierarchy of respiratory centers is justified here still remains to be fully determined. We refer to Samson Wright, *Applied Physiology,* 3d ed. (Oxford, 1929), p. 335: "Lumsden has recently reinvestigated the matter and has shown that the respiratory centre is a more complex structure than has hitherto been suspected. If the transsection is made in the *midbrain,* the breathing continues in normal fashion. As soon as the hinder limits of the inferior colliculi are passed and the action involves the *upper pons,* a new type of breathing appears. A slow deep inspiration is taken, and the inspiratory position of the chest is held for two or even three minutes. During the latter part of this inspiration the muscles slowly relax and finally give way suddenly and the air is expelled from the chest. Two or three relatively quick inspirations of abnormal type occur, and following these another prolonged inspiration appears. The cycle may repeat itself with great regularity for some hours, but the duration of the inspirations gradually lessens. These prolonged inspirations Lumsden refers to as *apneuses,* and this type of breathing can be called apneustic breathing. When the section is in the region of the *striae acusticae,* rhythmic respiration continues, but now consists of a series of *gasps.* Inspiration and expiration begin and end suddenly, and are followed by a pause. Division of the medulla oblongata at the level of the *calamus scriptorius* causes the cessation of all respiratory movements and death. To explain these phenomena, Lumsden postulates the presence of a series of centres in the lower brain stem, each of which is released if the centre above it is destroyed.

"The sequence of events in quiet respiration may be as follows: The gasping centre can be ignored, as it plays no part at all. The apneustic centre initiates the inspiratory movement, which is not allowed to continue for long, but is rapidly cut short by the higher pneumotaxic centre. Expiration is thus passive in character and is brought about by simple inhibition of inspiratory activity. The midbrain has no appreciable influence on respiration."

See also H. Rohracher, *Die Vorgänge im Gehirn und das geistige Leben* (Leipzig, 1939), p. 121: "The brain stem can further—and this is one of its principal functions—discharge and release. If, in the occurrence of excitations, *tensions* result from opposing states, then, following a certain maximum degree of intensity, there comes to be an *eruption:* explosive reactions, raging, screaming. In addition to these gross measures for the diversion of energy, the brain stem also knows more moderate ones. These take place, above all, in the following way: the excitations are directed to the lower centers in order that there they can expend their energy in activating the peripheral organs. An apparatus frequently employed for this is that of the secretion of tears: weeping. We assume for this purpose a center in the neighborhood of the ganglion nucleus for the VIIth cranial nerve, from which the nerve transmission travels to a ganglion nucleus located in the head (G. sphenopalatinum) and from there to the Nervus lacrimalis, the endings of which pass into the tear ducts. Since the mucous glands of the nasal passages are also provided for by G. sphenopalatinum, these glands also begin to secrete as soon as this center becomes excited. The remaining phenomena of weeping are probably brought about in this way: immediately adjacent to the lacrimal center are the Vth and VIIth cranial nerves; these, which lead to the musculature of the face, are likewise excited. Tears, of course, are introduced by characteristically convulsive movements and contortions of the musculature in the regions of the mouth and nose. But, in addition, the breathing center is to be found in the neighborhood of these ganglion nuclei, and from its participation presumably arise the curious disturbances of breathing found in weeping, which also produce the sound of sobbing. As soon as the tears flow, the cortical excitations speedily die away. . . . *Laughter* can also be alleviating. The mechanism which begins to function in this case and which produces the peculiar rhythmical sound of laughter is, however, still more complicated than that of weeping. Since we can also laugh voluntarily, the function of the brain stem is, therefore, not so clear."

No more precise reference is to be found in W. R. Hess, *Beiträge zur Physiologie des Hirnstammes. II: Das Zwischenhirn und die Regulation von Kreislauf und Atmung* (1938), nor in Wittkower, *Der Einfluss der Gemütsbewegungen auf den Körper* (Vienna-Leipzig, 1936), or W. H. von Wyss, "Einfluss psychischer Vorgänge auf Atmung, Pulsfrequenz, Blutdruck und Blutverteilung," *Handbuch der normalen und pathologischen Physiologie* (Berlin, 1931). For an understanding of the concept of stratification in the structure of man *as a whole* see E. Rothacker, *Die Schichten der Persönlichkeit* (Leipzig, 1938).

30. Out of the sparse literature on this subject, I mention H. Frank, *Zur Klinik der Pseudobulbärparalyse*, doctoral dissertation, Munich, 1927, and J. L. R. Pacaud, *Contribution à l'étude du mécanisme du rire*, doctoral dissertation, Nancy, 1928. In addition, cf. P. Bard, "The Neuro-humoral Basis of Emotional Reactions," *Handbook of General Experimental Psychology* (Worcester, Mass., 1934), pp. 264–311. Also important is the symptom-complex of multiple sclerosis. On the question of a "fit of laughter" (geloplegia) cf. A. Knapp, "Die Differentialdiagnose der Petit mal–Anfälle," *Der Nervenarzt*, XV, No. 1 (1942), p. 28.

31. Even the disorganization which comes to light in the reactions of laughing and crying must follow a principle of organization. Portmann makes the following observation: "Previous studies of laughing and crying give no reply to the question why these particu-

lar life-situations are answered with just these strange means of expression," i.e., life-situations "which it is no longer possible to master with the acquired means of controlled expression and intelligent action." And then he continues: "It would seem to me that the relation to the total form of existence which early ontogenesis encompasses at least allows the particular choice of means of expression to be somewhat more thoroughly understood. Early concentration of all responses on the vital sucking zone of the mouth enables us to understand that it is the seat of the primary means of social contact. We can further make intelligible that this means of expression in later life comes to be bound to situations which in early life correspond to the most common condition of unanswerableness" ("Die Biologie und das Phänomen des Geistigen," *Eranos-Jahrbuch*, XIV [1946], pp. 550–51).

A more comprehensive idea, to which otherwise familiar facts also attest, is that disorganization of behavior frequently appears as a lowering of levels, i.e., a falling-off of determinate forms of behavior which sympathetically involves the rest. By forcing down the level of differentiation on the whole, the falling-off in detail is reduced, or, if one will, disappears. The habitus becomes infantile. Or is it a question of genuine regression, of a true reversion to a childish level, or a reactivation of infantile possibilities through the suppression of inhibitions or drives which correspond to a more modulated behavior? Slipping-off (*if* it is such) into laughing and crying *also* takes place in the region of the mouth, but not there alone and not as the preferred region. The mobile middle region of the face follows the pulses of a "play of impulse" in which the respiratory apparatus (perhaps again only as an irradiative zone) has a share. In smiling, the matter is otherwise. Here, the expression seizes *on* the mouth. In laughing and crying, on the other hand, the mouth, like the eyes, must go along with these actions, so to speak. In my opinion, the convulsive eruption points to an origin other than that of the suckling mechanism.

Finally, we must ask ourselves the question whether, in early life, unanswerable situations predominate. The grown-up sees the helplessness of the child, but does the small child experience his situation in a corresponding way? Squalling and crying are also motor substitution forms for the absence of speech and can be appropriate for the child in both answerable and unanswerable situations. The categorical structure of the child's environment need *not* stand in disproportion to his speechlessness and evident helplessness, as measured by the standards of the grown-up. The *comparatively* minimal field of action of the infant affords him correspondingly limited possibilities of perception and hence of questioning. Thus we should not assume without further ado an excess of unanswerable situations for his consciousness. In any case, the value of Portmann's conception is not lessened by these considerations, even though the ontogenetic interpretation of the primitiveness of the unarticulated forms of expression—better, perhaps, forms of eruption—cannot be maintained. I am thankful to him for attempting to develop my theory further in a direction in which it still leaves most to be desired.

In addition, I must refer to two works which have appeared while I was preparing the first edition of this book: Joach. Ritter, "Über das Lachen," *Blätter für Deutsche Philosophie,* Nos. 1 and 2 (1940), and C. Leonhardt, "Die forensische Bedeutung des Weinens," *Arch. f. d. ges. Psych.*, CVII, Nos. 1 and 2 (1940). For the analysis of smiling cf. Buytendijk's lecture in Nymegen, *De eerste glimlach van het kind* (1947).

Index